DECAD

T0302733

Phil Collins
in the 1980s

Andrew Wild

SONICBOND

sonicbondpublishing.com

Sonicbond Publishing Limited
www.sonicbondpublishing.co.uk
Email: info@sonicbondpublishing.co.uk

First Published in the United Kingdom 2022
First Published in the United States 2022

British Library Cataloguing in Publication Data:
A Catalogue record for this book is available from the British Library

ISBN 978-1-78952-185-6

Typeset in ITC Garamond & ITC Avant Garde
Printed and bound in England

Graphic design and typesetting: Full Moon Media

DECADES

Phil Collins

in the 1980s

Andrew Wild

SONICBOND

sonicbondpublishing.com

Also by Andrew Wild

Local History

108 Steps Around Macclesfield (Sigma Press, 1994 / 2nd edition, Rumble Strips, 2018)
Exploring Chester (Sigma Press, 1996 / re-publication, Rumble Strips, 2018)
Ever Forward (MADS, 1997)

Biographies

Play On (Twelfth Night, 2009)
One For The Record (Avalon, 2013 / 2nd edition, 2018)

Music

Pink Floyd Song by Song (Fonthill, 2017)
Queen On Track (Sonicbond, 2018)
The Beatles: An A-Z Guide to Every Song (Sonicbond, 2019)
Solo Beatles 1969-1980 On Track (Sonicbond, 2020)
Crosby, Stills and Nash On Track (Sonicbond, 2020)
Dire Straits On Track (Sonicbond, 2021)
Fleetwood Mac in the 1970s (Sonicbond, 2021)
Eric Clapton Solo On Track (Sonicbond, 2021)
Eric Clapton Sessions On Track (Sonicbond, 2022)

Films

James Bond On Screen (Sonicbond, 2021)

Comics

The Perfect Marvel Comics Collection vol. 1: 1939-1965 (Rumble Strips, 2022)
The Perfect Marvel Comics Collection vol. 2: 1966-1973 (Rumble Strips, 2022)
The Perfect Marvel Comics Collection vol. 3: 1974-1985 (Rumble Strips, 2022)

Plays

The Difficult Crossing (Stagescripts, 2016)
A Difficult Man (Rumble Strips, 2021)

When you're a solo artist and simultaneously in a band … there's no time to stop and smell the roses, or to rue the failures and process them.
Phil Collins, *Not Dead Yet*, 2016

There is darkness in Phil Collins's music. There is also lightness. He is serious and silly, profound as well as puny, impressive and imbecilic, with enough excellence and embarrassment to round out a dozen lesser careers.
Steven Hyden, *The Ringer*, 2016

Unless noted otherwise, all direct quotes attributed to Phil Collins are taken from his 2016 autobiography *Not Dead Yet*.

This one is for my great pal Stuart Nicholson.

Acknowledgements

Thank you to Emma Roebuck for advice, wisdom, moral support and some missing tracks; to Stacy Doller for encouragement; to Brian Chatton and Phil Palmer for correspondence; to Anthony Rowsick for opening his address book; to Simon Collins for asking his Dad.

Thanks once again to Nick Jackson for peerless proofreading.

Would you like to write for Sonicbond Publishing?

At Sonicbond Publishing we are always on the look-out for authors, particularly for our two main series:

On Track. Mixing fact with in depth analysis, the On Track series examines the work of a particular musical artist or group. All genres are considered from easy listening and jazz to 60s soul to 90s pop, via rock and metal.

On Screen. This series looks at the world of film and television. Subjects considered include directors, actors and writers, as well as entire television and film series. As with the On Track series, we balance fact with analysis.

While professional writing experience would, of course, be an advantage the most important qualification is to have real enthusiasm and knowledge of your subject. First-time authors are welcomed, but the ability to write well in English is essential.

Sonicbond Publishing has distribution throughout Europe and North America, and all books are also published in E-book form. Authors will be paid a royalty based on sales of their book.

Further details are available from www.sonicbondpublishing.co.uk. To contact us, complete the contact form there or email info@sonicbondpublishing.co.uk

DECADES | Phil Collins in the 1980s

Contents

Introduction

On 28 June 1987, the day after my 21st birthday, I made my way out of Roundhay Park in Leeds after a gig by the globally-massive 1980s version of Genesis. I saw a lad, not much older than me, sobbing. 'The Americans did that to them', he cried.

And then, thirty-four years later, in August 2021, my mate Jules and I saw the terrific band G2 Definitive Genesis in the Devil's Arse cavern in Castleton, Derbyshire. G2 play Genesis' music from 1970 through to 1980, tending towards the *Seconds Out* era of 1976-1977. The demographic was very clear. 'Does anyone here remember the 1970s?' asked singer Dave Whitehouse at one point. 'Is anyone here *in* their 70s?' During the interval, I overheard one punter complain that although the band was good, 'the singer sounds too much like Phil Collins…'

And herein lies the rub. Phil Collins' work as a vocalist, songwriter and drummer with Genesis and as a solo act is somehow inferior to the earlier Genesis lineup with singer Peter Gabriel. The band's work from 1970 to 1975 is often preserved in aspic as the 'real' Genesis. It seems that many fans of a music labelled 'progressive' have not allowed Genesis to, well, progress. But progress they did – to a massive selling behemoth through the 1980s and beyond. Collins' parallel solo career is equally noteworthy. And yet Collins' solo music is still disparaged by many as lightweight music 'for housewives'. In my view, there's room for everything – that Genesis included both 'Easy Lover' and 'Supper's Ready' on a 2014 compilation album suggests that they agree.

It is true that Phil Collins was everywhere in the 1980s. He had more top forty singles in the US than any other artist during the 1980s: fourteen as a solo artist and eleven with Genesis, along with two number one albums. Add to this twenty-five solo/group hit singles and eight number one albums in the UK He also recorded with artists as diverse as Peter Gabriel, John Martyn, Jack Lancaster, Brian Chatton, Rupert Hine, Frida, Robert Plant, Gary Brooker, Mike Oldfield, Ralph McTell, Marti Webb, Al Di Meola, Adam Ant, Eric Clapton, Phil Bailey, Band Aid, Marilyn Martin, Howard Jones, Paul McCartney, Tina Turner, Chaka Khan, Boys Don't Cry, The Four Tops, Stephen Bishop and Tears For Fears. That's another thirty-five albums or standalone singles, some of which were massive global hits.

He also found time, somehow, to tour with Plant and Clapton in addition to his extensive in-concert duties with Genesis and as a solo artist. And perform at Live Aid. At both concerts. That's around six hundred live concerts in total between 1980 and 1989. There's no doubt that the guy was busy during that period!

Amidst the overwhelming commercial success and ahead of any other career plan, Phil Collins was and is a musician. His ubiquity between 1980 and 1989 hides ten years of magnificent music. This book examines Phil Collins' musical output through these ten tumultuous years.

Before 1980

Philip David Charles Collins was born on 30 January 1951 in Putney, west London, ten miles east of the family home in Whitton, not far from Twickenham. They moved to nearby Hounslow – at that time the last stop on the Piccadilly Line – when Collins was four years old. A precocious talent, he started playing on a homemade drum kit aged five.

He bought his first 'real' kit from Albert's Music Shop in Twickenham in 1963. A thirteen-year-old Phil Collins is pictured sitting at that kit on the cover of the 2010 album, *Going Back*.

He said in *Interview* Magazine in March 1983:

> My brother was eight or nine years older and he was always listening to Radio Luxembourg which played Bill Haley, Eddie Cochran, stuff like that, which didn't interest me at all. I never ever liked that music, but when I started playing seriously, the English beat thing was just happening, the Shadows and bands like that. It was the very early '60s. I remember buying *Please Please Me*. I used to put the record player on very loud and set up my drums, so I was facing the mirror; that way you don't look at what you're doing. Then when I was fourteen, I went to a teacher to learn to read drum music. I figured when this rock-and-roll thing finished, I would have to make a living playing in a dance band or in an orchestra pit. So I learned to read drum music, but I found that my capacity for reading was not anywhere near as good as actually playing by instinct. I would have this chart in front of me and my teacher would have me play it and I'd play it very haltingly. I'd get exasperated and I'd ask him to play it and he'd play it and I'd say, 'Oh you mean that!' and I would repeat it perfectly. Give it to me written down and I had no idea. So I decided to abandon that area of learning and ever since, I've lived off my wits musically.

Collins was also developing an interest in acting and began professional lessons at the Barbara Speake Stage School in East Acton. His mother, June, established a talent agency around this time, supplying, as Phil recalls, 'all-singing, all-dancing children to London's West End, and to the blossoming commercial TV and film world'.

After appearing as an extra in *A Hard Day's Night* in spring 1964, Collins' first major role arrived later that year as the Artful Dodger in the stage musical *Oliver!*, where he replaced future Monkee Davy Jones. The musical had opened in 1960 and would run for over 2,600 performances. Collins would perform in the show for seven months, earning £15 each week.

'This is a big part,' he writes. 'The entrance of The Artful Dodger is the moment when the show lifts. This tale of Victorian workhouses and grinding poverty is pretty much doom and despair till the chirpy, light-fingered urchin comes on and sings 'Consider Yourself'. Consider, too, that the Dodger also sings wonderful, now-timeless songs like 'I'd Do Anything' and 'Be Back Soon' with his gang. They're my first lead vocals, and I relish performing them eight times a week.'

Collins retired from the role when his voice broke but returned as the bullying Noah Claypole in 1969. By then, he had formed his first band, the soul-influenced The Real Thing, and became a regular visitor to the Marquee Club in Soho.

Collins recalled almost fifty years later:

> The Marquee evening performance schedule usually goes like this; support band, headliner, support band again, headliner again. I can usually see the first three, but have to leave before the final headliner's set so I can catch the train that gets me home in time for my curfew of 10:30 p.m. Then, on 24 January 1967, Jimi Hendrix plays the Marquee for the first time. The first of the American guitarist's four legendary shows there, this will go down in the annals of rock history as one of the epochal rock shows of the sixties. I'm first in line to get in, nab a front-row seat…but then in frustration, have to leave before Hendrix comes on. The last train to the end of the line is calling.

Hooking up with local musician Ronnie Caryl, Collins played a season at Pontins in Paignton, Collins performed at several American army bases in Norfolk and Cambridgeshire as part a semi-professional R & B band called The Charge and sat in with both The Cliff Charles Blues Band and The Freehold. Collins and Caryl formed a four-piece, Hickory, who recorded a few demos in early 1968. One of these, 'Lying, Crying Dying', was rediscovered in the 2010s.

By 1969, Hickory had been renamed Flaming Youth. They recorded one album, *Ark 2*. Keyboard player Brian Chatton would employ Phil Collins as a session musician in the 1980s.

Collins subsequently auditioned for Vinegar Joe and Manfred Mann Chapter Three and attended sessions for George Harrison's *All Things Must Pass*. 'As the seventies dawn,' he writes, 'and with it the end of my first year of adulthood, I'm foraging for food, money and a future. I've been in a few bands, none of which have come to anything. I'm hungry, but I'm still stuck in Hounslow and all that goes with living at the end of the line. I need a full-time gig, or a better gig, or preferably both.'

Meanwhile, the rock band Genesis had formed in 1967 at Charterhouse School in Surrey. They released *From Genesis To Revelation* in March 1969 with thc line-up of Tony Banks, Mike Rutherford, Peter Gabriel, Anthony Phillips and a series of drummers. Phillips left in July 1970 after completion of recording sessions for their second album *Trespass,* which included the tour de force track 'The Knife'. Drummer John Mayhew was asked to step aside. 'We decided that if we were to continue after Ant left,' Tony Banks wrote on the Genesis' website after Mayhew's death in 2009, 'we had to find a more creative drummer, a hard decision because by this time, John had become a friend.'

'I just technically wasn't good enough,' Mayhew admitted, 'that's the truth of the matter'.

Genesis advertised for a drummer and guitarist in *Melody Maker* with contact details for their manager, Tony Stratton-Smith. Collins through his regular visits to the Marquee, knew Stratton-Smith and tracked him down with a view to talking himself into Genesis. He was invited to audition and, with pal Ronnie Caryl, headed to the Gabriel family's 'oversized, beautiful country pile'.

Collins describes what happened next in his memoirs.

> I ring the bell, and a distinguished-looking, middle-aged woman opens the door. Somehow Mrs. Gabriel works out that we're not here to sell Encyclopædia Britannica or join her bridge circle. We must be here to try out for her son's pop group. 'Oh, do come in,' she says, smiling. 'You're a little early. Please feel free to have a swim while you're waiting.'
>
> It's posh with a capital p.We've arrived a couple of drummers early and, as I'm splashing about, I hear my rivals go through their paces. The standard is decent and I quickly appreciate what I'm up against.

Collins was able to listen to the audition pieces and with his acute musical ear, he was ready when his time came.

Collins says: 'I later learn that Peter knew the moment I sat down that I was the guy; seemingly the assured way I set up my kit was telling. Mike was less convinced. Tony felt quietly confident. History does not record the opinion of Mrs. Gabriel.'

'By the time it came to Phil's turn,' Mike Rutherford writes in his own memoirs, 'he'd already heard and memorised the part we were using for the audition and, when he sat down at the kit, you just knew. He had confidence. All the other guys had fiddled around, moved the cymbals, shifted their seat about a bit, but Phil simply changed the snare round because he was left-handed and got on with it.'

Collins, recognisably a versatile and skilled drummer, received the call telling him he had got the job on 8 August 1970. Ronnie Caryl was not a good fit and wasn't taken on. Genesis would be a four-piece for several weeks and performed several gigs in this format: their first was at Medway College in Chatham on 2 October, promoting the newly-released *Trespass*. They recruited guitarist Mick Barnard later that month, and Ronnie Caryl also helped, but the band's 'classic' line-up was completed in early 1971 when Genesis enlisted Steve Hackett.

Hackett had placed a small ad in *Melody Maker,* which read: 'Imaginative Guitarist/Writer seeks involvement with receptive musicians, determined to strive beyond existing stagnant music forms.'

Trespass would creep into the lower reaches of the UK album charts. Subsequent releases would be incrementally more successful: *Nursery Cryme* (November 1971, UK number 39), *Foxtrot* (October 1972, UK number 12), *Genesis Live* (July 1973, UK number 9), *Selling England By The Pound* (October 1973, UK number 3; US number 70) and the ambitious double album *The Lamb Lies Down On Broadway* (November 1974, UK number 10; US number 41). During this period, Genesis were very much regarded as a key band in the UK progressive rock scene, alongside Yes, Pink Floyd, King Crimson and others. Tracks such as 'Stagnation', 'The Musical Box', 'The Fountain Of Salmacis', 'Watcher Of The Skies', 'Dancing With The Moonlit Knight', 'The Cinema Show', 'In The Cage', 'Back In N.Y.C.', 'Counting Out Time', 'The Carpet Crawlers', 'The Colony Of Slippermen' and particularly 'Firth Of Fifth' and 'Supper's Ready' laid down a standard for a musical genre that was particularly fertile during this period.

> In terms of progressive rock, 'Supper's Ready' ticked all the boxes. Apart from its strong tunes, and adventurous arrangements and playing, there was a hip 'otherness' about the group, an eccentricity and a sardonic sense of humour with Peter Gabriel the increasingly charismatic frontman. There was also something quite clever about Genesis, which was droll without being smug.
>
> Michael Barnes, *A New Day Yesterday*, 2020

But Peter Gabriel wanted a change of direction and officially left Genesis in August 1975 after an ostentatious and challenging tour where the band performed their latest album in its entirety, with slides, backdrop, costumes and lights.

Genesis subsequently advertised: 'Singer wanted for Genesis-type group'.

'We're looking in a leisurely manner,' Collins told the British music weekly *Sounds*. As he wrote later:

> We get all sorts. We whittle them down to a presentable bunch before we start auditioning. We're not just looking for someone with the vocal chops. We're asking ourselves, will he be a good writing partner? What will he bring to the band? We audition for five or six weeks. It's starting to become tedious. With the clock ticking we have no option but to commit to studio time. I say, 'How about I have a go?' And the rest of the guys shrug: 'Might as well.'… Mike and Tony later tell me it's like one of those cartoon lightbulb moments. They look at each other in the control room and their eyebrows say it all: By George, I think he's got it!

This move surprised everyone except, perhaps, Collins himself. He had sung backing and co-lead vocals on a number of Genesis album tracks, and taken the sole lead on the contemplative 'For Absent Friends' (*Nursery Cryme*) and its companion piece, the fragile 'More Fool Me' (*Selling England By The Pound*). Never lacking confidence, Collins' fit as a lead singer seems completely obvious today.

Collins, interviewed by *The Guardian* in 2021, said:

> I did enjoy it. I set out what I would do and what I wouldn't do. I personally felt that some of the visuals, the costumes and so on, were getting in the way of the vocals. I didn't think I'd be very good at doing that theatrical stuff anyway. So I said: 'Look, I can sing the songs, but anything else will be a bit of a question mark.'

'There was something fleeting about Gabriel,' wrote Philip Kamin and Peter Goddard in 1984. 'Something shadowy and magical and mysterious surrounding what he did. In contrast, there's something definite and compact and power-packed about Collins.'

Genesis' seventh album, *A Trick of the Tail* (1976) opens with the mighty 'Dance On A Volcano', a dyed-in-the-wool progressive rock track. Collins also shines on the gorgeous 'Ripples', perhaps the first flowering of the band's more commercial sound that developed over the next few albums. *A Trick of the Tail* rose to number 3 in the UK and number 31 in the US. Issues around stage performances would be solved by recruiting ex-Yes, ex-King Crimson drummer Bill Bruford for live shows. Collins also found time to record two albums and perform concerts with the British jazz-fusioners Brand X.

1977's *Wind & Wuthering* includes Rutherford's plaintive 'Your Own Special Way', brilliantly sung by Phil Collins. It was the band's first charting single in the US, 'the start of a tickle', as Rutherford described it. Likewise, Banks' 'Afterglow' ends the album on an anthemic high – the song would remain in the band's set for years.

The same year's *Spot The Pigeon* E.P., with its lead track 'Match Of The Day', would give Genesis their first UK top 20 single. The powerful and energetic double live album *Seconds Out*, recorded in June 1977, was the last Genesis album to feature Steve Hackett. It is perhaps the definitive statement from this short-lived iteration of Genesis and reclaims the Gabriel-era back catalogue for the new line-up.

With Hackett gone, Collins, Banks and Rutherford continued as a trio and began to move further from their progressive rock roots. Whilst longer, more complex songs would always form part of the Genesis catalogue, their albums now added a more radio-friendly pop-rock sound to their shorter songs. This strategy was immediately successful when the uplifting pop ballad 'Follow You Follow Me' – released in February 1978 and taken from *…And Then There Were Three…* – became their first UK Top 10 and US Top 40 single.

'I had nothing to do with 'Follow You Follow Me',' Phil Collins told *Rolling Stone* in 2016. 'It was written around a guitar piece by Mike. Tony wrote the words, which I didn't hear until the day I went in to record them. It was our first real hit. Genesis had been trying desperately to write pop singles for a long time. Everybody was a fan of the Beatles and the Kinks and the Stones, but we didn't have a very good editor in the band — it was hard to write songs shorter than ten minutes. But 'Follow You Follow Me' was a game-changer.'

> I always felt we were lucky to be the last ones left standing. Our competitors – people like Yes and ELP – had faded by that point. So we were the last of that prog bastion. We actually had our first hit record – 'Follow You Follow Me' – during the height of punk. It kind of carried us through that time.
>
> Tony Banks, *The Guardian*, September 2021

Banks' stirring, elegant love song 'Many Too Many', superbly sung by Collins, is another pointer to the song construction and vocal performances of Genesis in the 1980s. Banks later declared that 'making *...And Then There Were Three...* was a very pleasurable experience. We weren't in each other's way because we had such definite roles — we felt very complete in the studio.'

After a lengthy tour, close to one hundred shows between March and December 1978, Genesis went on hiatus to enable Collins' to address his relationship with his wife Andrea, which had become strained through his extensive absences from home. Banks and Rutherford recorded their debut solo albums *A Curious Feeling* (released October 1979, UK number 21) and *Smallcreep's Day* (released February 1980, UK number 13), both recorded at Abba's new Polar Studios in Stockholm. Phil Collins worked with Brand X and wrote several new songs of his own, mostly documenting the emotions of a failed marriage.

'Up until *...And Then There Were Three...* I was married with two kids and had a lot of other responsibilities,' Collins explained to Philip Kamin and Peter Goddard in 1984. 'I had to divide my time between what I had to do with my family and what I wanted to do with my musical career. The music tended to occupy at lot of space in my life, but I wasn't giving everything I had to it. So when my divorce happened I then ended up with all this extra time... and inclination to channel my energy into something – writing songs. When the situation came around where I could actually write ... and let my feelings flow through – then it all came out.'

This batch of songs was put to one side, for now. 'By the time we begin work on *Duke*,' Collins said later, 'I'm a little protective of these compositions.'

Genesis regrouped in Collins' master bedroom/home studio for writing sessions in October 1979 ahead of sessions in Stockholm the following month to record their next album, *Duke*.

Part One – Getting There

1980

Duke

Personnel:
Tony Banks: keyboards, backing vocals, 12-string guitar
Mike Rutherford: guitars, bass guitar, bass pedals, backing vocals
Phil Collins: drums, vocals, drum machine, percussion, duck
Recorded November–December 1979 at Polar, Stockholm, Sweden.
Produced by David Hentschel and Genesis
Album release: 28 March 1980.
Highest chart placings: UK: 1, US: 11
Side one: 'Behind The Lines', 'Duchess', 'Guide Vocal', 'Man of Our Times', 'Misunderstanding', 'Heathaze'
Side two: 'Turn It On Again', 'Alone Tonight', 'Cul-de-sac', 'Please Don't Ask', 'Duke's Travels', 'Duke's End'

'Turn It On Again' b/w 'Behind The Lines part 2'

UK single release: 8 March 1980. Highest chart position: 8.

'Duchess' b/w 'Open Door'

UK single release: 9 May 1980. Highest chart position: 46.

'Misunderstanding' b/w 'Behind The Lines'

US single release: 10 May 1980. Highest chart position: 14.

'Turn It On Again (remix)' b/w 'Evidence Of Autumn'

US single release: August 1980. Highest chart position: 58.

'Misunderstanding' b/w 'Evidence Of Autumn'

UK single release: 5 September 1980. Highest chart position: 42.

> By 1980, Genesis had adopted a more commercial approach to their music while retaining the signature elements that made the band unique. Banks' skill with harmony, Rutherford's craft with a tune and Collins' innovative rhythms and melodic sensibilities were perfectly matched to create a blend that none of them could create on their own.
> Steve Aldous, *The Songs of Genesis*, 2020

> We started writing as a group again, which used to bring all those magical moments. We hadn't really had those for a long time.
> Mike Rutherford, *Trouser Press*, 1982

> Having negotiated Peter Gabriel's abdication, they sailed out of debt and off towards international stardom, by-passing punk en route.
> Michael Barnes, *A New Day Yesterday*, 2020

> Just when it seemed that 'progressive rock' bands were on their way out, Genesis were entering an astonishing new phase that would be full of surprises and see them attain a worldwide following on a massive scale.
> Chris Welch, *Genesis: The Complete Guide To Their Music,* 2005

By the time they began to write and record *Duke*, Genesis had successfully moved beyond their early years. For better or worse, *Duke* marks the end of the dominating 'progressive' period in Genesis' music: the album signals a definitive switch from the artsy intellectualism of intricate, lengthy songs to something much more radio-friendly (and profitable).

Each of their remaining albums with Phil Collins would move further, incrementally, from 'Supper's Ready' to 'I Can't Dance'. There would always be space on future Genesis albums for longer, more complex pieces, but they were written and presented more often with a commercial hook: 'Abacab' and 'Dodo'/'Lurker' on *Abacab*, Home By The Sea' and 'Second Home By The Sea' on *Genesis*, 'The Brazilian' and 'Domino' on *Invisible Touch* and 'Driving The Last Spike' and 'Fading Lights' on *We Can't Dance*. These share the same DNA as 'Return Of The Giant Hogweed' and 'The Knife', but follow a different evolutionary path.

The reason for this clear change in direction is obvious: Genesis wanted to have hit singles, their appetites whetted by 'Follow You Follow Me'. This strategy was led by the workaholic Collins who was always involved in multiple projects, with a failed marriage as a result. It's easy to assume that Phil Collins' work ethic was driven by a need to compartmentalise his life – if he was perpetually busy with work, he had a reason to not address his personal demons. He also had a huge backlog of songs: *Duke* includes the first two songs to be credited solely to Phil Collins as a writer, 'Please Don't Ask' and 'Misunderstanding', .

'On this album, I put up two of my songs for the first time,' Collins told BBC Radio One's Kid Jensen in March 1980. 'Up until last year, I didn't write anything on my own and last year, I wrote a lot of songs.'

Whether the already-written 'In The Air Tonight' was presented to the rest of the band at these sessions has never been resolved. Collins said he did; Banks says not.

On 13 March, Genesis made their first appearance on the long-running BBC show *Top Of The Pops* to mime to their new single 'Turn It On Again'. The song entered the charts a few days later for a ten-week run, peaking at number eight. In the first week of April Collins' and Rutherford's appearance on the kids' TV programme TISWAS perhaps underlines their willingness to push for commercial success. It's impossible to imagine Steve Hackett or Peter Gabriel agreeing to ritual humiliation in pink leotards on live TV. Perhaps it was a step too far for Tony Banks who stayed away. 'Turn It On Again', 'Duchess' and 'Misunderstanding' were duly released as singles from *Duke*, although only the former would crack the top ten in the UK 'Misunderstanding' reached a creditable fourteen in the US – it's no coincidence that Genesis' first top twenty chart entry was a song written solely by Phil Collins

Duke was recorded at Abba's new Polar Studios in Stockholm in November and December 1979 and mixed at London's Maison Rouge Studios in January 1980.

'Behind The Lines' opens the album with a brilliant, confident fanfare which has a powerful, bright vocal from Phil Collins. *Duke* was his fourth album as lead vocalist and he had now, literally, found his voice. 'I've put more power and guts into my vocals', Collins told *Sounds* in May 1980. 'I had to take a crash course in singing … but now I'm moving into overdrive.'

> When he sang ['Behind The Lines']… it's not just that he's got a better voice than me—all the kind of embellishments and tales and things that happened on it just transformed it completely from being something like a session guy might do to something that a singer does and his own character is right across it for that reason. The resultant effect is very, very strong.
> Tony Banks, DVD interview, 2006

'Behind The Lines' moves seamlessly into the soulful, airy 'Duchess', one of Genesis' best songs of the period and which again includes excellent singing from Collins. This track opens with the very fresh sound of the chattering CR-78 drum machine first heard on the Brand X song 'Wal to Wal' from 1979's *Product*. The very presence of this new technology liberated the band's songwriting as all three writers could and would use drum machines to demo ideas for rhythms and structures.

'I use the CR-78 on 'Duchess'', Collins wrote in his memoirs, 'I've used it on my demos, and after a year in my bedroom with it, I know what it can and can't do. It's incredibly limited, but it works really well on 'Duchess'.'

> One of the finest tracks in the entire Genesis discography, 'Duchess' [tells] the story of a diva's rise and fall, with Collins' soulful vocal powered by Banks's driving piano chords and some truly colossal drums. For all its anthemic qualities, however, [the] most bewitching moments came with its intro and outro: ambient, elemental passages of programmed electronic drums that suggest the band were paying attention to the experimental work of Brian Eno. Along with Banks's restrained synths, the drum machine pulses conjure a hypnotic and evocative soundscape that was airy and futuristic.
> Stevie Chick, *The Guardian*, 2014

Released as a single in May 1980, the heavily edited version of 'Duchess' feels ripped out from the music that surrounds it. The entertaining video was filmed at the Liverpool Empire at the beginning of May.

Banks' short, emotional 'Guide Vocal' was unlike anything else in Genesis' back catalogue and could easily have come from the forthcoming *Face Value*.

These three songs comprise not only a superb opening to *Duke* but also the first thirteen minutes of the 'Duke Suite'. Originally planned as a side-long series of interconnected songs, the various sections were split across the album as the band did not want comparisons with the likes of 'Supper's Ready'. This decision was made early in the recording process: the order in which the songs were recorded suggests that the idea of a side-long suite was ditched ahead of any studio sessions. In concert, however, 'Duke's Suite' formed the centrepiece of the band's concerts in 1980: 'Behind The Lines', 'Duchess', 'Guide Vocal', 'Turn It On Again', 'Duke's Travels' and 'Dukes End'. This sequence remains one of Genesis' most powerful musical statements. The mighty pairing of 'Duke's Travels' and 'Duke's End' reprises musical themes from 'Behind The Lines', 'Guide Vocal' and 'Turn It On Again'. It includes a guitar solo that is pure Steve Hackett and also plays a wry musical tribute to King Crimson's 'In The Court Of The Crimson King'.

Collins in 2016: 'We know a single piece of that length is only going to be compared to 'Supper's Ready' so we opt not to go there again. It's a new decade and maybe 'suites' that take up a whole side of an album won't be indulged quite so readily anymore.'

That might be a touch of revisionism. With the suite on side one, side two would have contained four ballads running five minutes each along with 'Misunderstanding' and 'Man of Our Times': hardly a sensible balance for a two-sided record album.

The big hit, the classic 'Turn It On Again', started as a slow guitar riff in loping 13/8 time signature. The riff was written by Mike Rutherford for his solo album but remained unused. It was added to a Tony Banks chord progression, then Collins suggested speeding it up, adding synthesised horns and a snappy drum arrangement. The lyrics are Rutherford's. Despite its complexity, 'Turn It On Again' was catchy enough to head into the UK top ten when it was released as Genesis' first single of the 1980s. An edited version of 'Behind The Lines' comprised the b-side. 'Turn It On Again' entered the band's setlist and has been performed at every Genesis gig since, even those in Phil Collins' ten-year interregnum.

Rutherford's tough, powerful 'Man Of Our Times' suggests the synthesiser riff from Gary Numan's 'Cars', released the previous summer. The simple, direct 'Misunderstanding' has a looping beat similar to a song by Toto. The influence of their big hit 'Hold The Line' is clear. 'Misunderstanding' shares many common features, including the off-kilter drums, the rising guitar phrases and the tinkling piano. Both 'Hot Sun In The Summertime' by Sly and the Family Stone (1969) and 'Sail On Sailor' by The Beach Boys (1973) provide further strong influences on this underrated, soulful pop song. 'Misunderstanding' was Genesis' biggest US hit single to date. Collins' original demo recorded in 1979 has been released on the deluxe version of *Face Value* – all of the music and melodies are in place, but the lyrics are yet to be written.

Banks' 'Heathaze' and 'Cul-De-Sac' are hangovers of the band's late-70s prog explorations. Collins does not sound totally engaged in both songs, with their oblique lyrics diametrically opposite to the simpler pieces he had been writing in recent months. Both songs are, as you might expect, musically beautiful, with keyboards prominent, lots of dynamics and, on 'Cul-De-Sac', some jazzy drumming.

'Alone Tonight' and 'Please Don't Ask' are close in mood. Rutherford's low-key 'Alone Tonight' has a close-miked vocal, shimmering guitars, a heartfelt vocal and one of Rutherford's brilliantly uplifting choruses.

'Please Don't Ask' was selected from the demos that Phil Collins had written at home during 1979. This demo was first heard publicly as part of a radio interview in 1981 and this radio broadcast was included on the 2016 reissue of *Face Value*. The song gives an idea of how *Face Value* might have sounded with Banks' and Rutherford's involvement with its gleaming keyboards and busy guitar. 'Please Don't Ask' has very personal lyrics, tender vocals and a solo-era Collins chorus. Genesis' decision to select 'Misunderstanding' and 'Please Don't Ask' from Collins' batch of songs was a key development in bringing the band closer to global commercial success: bipartisan listeners could relate to songs such as these and they sounded great on the radio.

The British weekly *New Musical Express* were, however, extremely direct in their review.

> The more personal numbers are dogged by an emotional impotence that's caused less by cruel circumstance than by the complacency of a pampered personality. *Duke* is an innately conservative album. There's the snobbish connotations of the title; the group's strict adherence to their old musical form; and, inherent in the lyrics, the preaching of the cocooned commentator who has internalised his disappointment and made a virtue out of a pessimism that is the ultimate, escapist protection. More profoundly depressing that this album is the thought that the group are a habit that thousands can't kick. If Genesis had any guts they'd give up.
> Lynn Hanna, *NME*, 5 April 1980

Duke entered the UK chart at number one the week of its release in April 1980, the first of five consecutive Genesis studio albums to reach number one in the UK. Initially mastered with quite a brittle sound, the *Genesis 1976–1982* box set includes a magnificent new stereo mix.

Two outtakes were released as b-sides in 1980. Rutherford's gorgeous 'Open Door', despite its elegance, was perhaps too close to *Wind & Wuthering*-era Genesis to be considered as part of *Duke*. Banks' 'Evidence Of Autumn' is a moody piece which was possibly too fragmented for the mood of the music on *Duke*. It was most likely dropped in favour of 'Cul-De-Sac'.

Phil Collins and Mike Rutherford were interviewed by Nicky Horne at Capitol Radio on 5 February 1980. Horne was a long-time supporter of Genesis. Album tracks from *Duke* (still six weeks away from release) and *Smallcreep's Day* play alongside interview topics which included the composition and recording of Duke and Phil's forthcoming solo album. Collins, remarkably, allows the broadcast of two of his demos: 'Misunderstanding' and a brand new recording of 'Tomorrow Never Knows'. This remains the only place to hear Phil's solo demo of the track that would be included on *Face Value.*

Duke Tour

An eight-week UK series of shows between March and May 1980 was the last Genesis theatre tour before they moved to arenas and stadia. It offered a perfectly balanced setlist of old 'prog' Genesis and the more pop-orientated band they were to become. At most venues, the band performed 'Deep In The Motherlode', 'Dancing With The Moonlit Knight (opening section)', 'The Carpet Crawlers', 'Squonk', 'One For The Vine', 'Behind The Lines', 'Duchess', 'Guide Vocal', 'Turn It On Again', 'Duke's Travels', Duke's End', 'Say It's Alright Joe', 'The Lady Lies', 'Ripples', 'In The Cage', 'The Colony Of Slippermen' (instrumental excerpt), 'Afterglow', 'Follow You Follow Me', 'Dance On A Volcano', 'Drum Duet' and 'Los Endos' with 'I Know What I Like (In My Wardrobe)' as the encore. 'Misunderstanding', 'The Knife' and 'Back In NYC' were also played at around half of the dates.

Collins performed a one-off gig with John Martyn at the Bournemouth Winter Gardens on 14 March ahead of the opening dates of the latest Genesis concert tour.

As the UK *Duke* live shows drew to a close, Genesis played three concerts at London venues: 5 May at the Theatre Royal, Drury Lane and 6-7 May at the Lyceum. All three shows were recorded to 24-track audio. Edited sets were supplied to the BBC and to Capital Radio for broadcast. In addition, the two Lyceum dates were filmed by the BBC. These master recordings have produced a slow trickle of official releases. 'One For The Vine' from Drury Lane is available on *Three Sides Live*, released in 1982. 'Deep In The Motherlode' from this same concert is on *Archive #2* (2000). This same set includes three songs from the Lyceum: 'Ripples', 'Duke's Travels' and 'The Lady Lies'. 'Follow You Follow Me' from the Lyceum is on *Three Sides Live*. A different recording of 'The Lady Lies' was released on a flexi-disc given away to readers of Flexipop magazine in August 1982. Seven other songs from this concert are included on a DVD in the *1976-1982* box set (2007), namely 'Behind The Lines', 'Duchess', 'Guide Vocal', 'In The Cage', 'Afterglow', 'Dance On A Volcano' and 'Los Endos'.

In total, these disparate sources comprise around one-third of the songs performed. A BBC rebroadcast in December 1980 generated a highly popular and very high-quality bootleg release which is a must-listen for any Genesis fan: this is arguably Genesis at their performance peak.

The six-week US tour from mid-May to late June was notable for Collins' meeting his future wife Jill Tavelman in Los Angeles, after Genesis had played the Greek Theatre.

Peter Gabriel, QE2, Grace and Danger

Peter Gabriel's third self-titled solo album was recorded in the second half of 1979 at Townhouse Studios in west London. Built and owned by Virgin Records, Townhouse was a busy studio with a new solid-state recording console and a very lively 'stone room' for natural reverb. Phil Collins plays on several tracks on the album, but it is the opening 'Intruder' which heralded the drum sound that threatened to dominate the 1980s.

The Townhouse's staff engineer was Hugh Padgham. 'One day Phil was playing in the studio,' Padgham recalled in an interview with ProSound.com in 2018, 'And I inadvertently pressed the talkback button [which allowed those in the control room to hear and speak to the musicians in the studio]. Out came this ginormous sound, which everyone in the control room said sounded incredible. They all said, 'Let's have a bit of that on something', but the problem was that because the talkback was built into the desk, it couldn't be recorded.'

The studio's maintenance engineers found a solution and this new effect was played to Peter Gabriel, who immediately wrote 'Intruder' around a drum pattern played by Collins. 'We started recording and almost for a laugh, I switched in a noise gate,' Padgham said. 'That's where the cut-off sound came from. So we now had something that sounded enormous but with no die away.'

And thus was born the distinctive drum sound of 'In The Air Tonight', 'Against All Odds (Take A Look At Me Now)', 'Do You Know, Do You Care', 'I Wish It Would Rain Down', 'You'll Be In My Heart', 'Mama' and 'No Son Of Mine'. Padgham would deploy this characteristic effect on several songs on XTC's *Drums and Wires and Black Sea* recorded in 1980. Duran Duran used a similar technique on 'The Wild Boys' (1984) and 'A View To A Kill' (1985). Bruce Springsteen used it on 'Born in the USA' (1984), as did The Power Station ('Some Like It Hot') and Kate Bush ('Hounds of Love') in 1985.

Phil Collins would return to the Townhouse to record his four solo albums of the 1980s, as well as production sessions for John Martyn and Eric Clapton.

Peter Gabriel was released on 30 May 1980, with 'Intruder' as the opening track. Completists will need the German version with re-recorded vocals: 'Intruder' becomes 'Eindringling'.

Mike Oldfield's sixth album, *QE2*, was released five months later. It was recorded at his new home studio in Denham, Buckinghamshire.

> For the next album, I decided I needed people to work with, as I couldn't work on my own any more, so I asked [head of Virgin Records] Simon Draper if he knew anyone. Simon suggested an engineer-producer called David Hentschel, who had produced some of the early Genesis albums. I met with David and got on very well with him. I thought he was very talented, he gave a lot of helpful input and it was nice to work with someone new. I had a few guests on there, like Phil Collins, who came and did some drums.

Mike Oldfield, *Changeling,* 2007

David Hentschel had worked as engineer or co-producer on several Genesis albums. In addition, Oldfield's percussionist on these sessions Morris Pert had recorded and toured with Phil Collins as a member of Brand X in 1976. Presumably, Pert's credit on the original vinyl release *Moroccan Roll* is coincidental, as it reads: 'percussion and a vast number of bits and things that he hit while the tape was running, including: the QE2, Idi Amin, and undiscovered parts of Scotland'.

Exact recording dates are unavailable, but as Oldfield was on tour between mid-April and late July, and again in the last two weeks of September, it seems likely that sessions took place in August 1980. *QE2* was released on 31 October 1980.

Collins appears on the album's opening tracks 'Taurus 1' and 'Sheba'. The former opens with the familiar sound of the CR 'Compu-Rhythm' drum machine. Collins had used it on *Duke* and on the in-progress *Face Value.* He also adds his distinctive kit work in the first third of this lengthy, shifting instrumental. The mesmerising 'Sheba' has some huge tom-tom fills and Collins' characteristic cymbal work.

The previous May, Phil Collins had been employed as the drummer and occasional backing vocalist on the album *Grace and Danger* by the mercurial John Martyn. Recorded at the Dick James' Music Studios in Holborn, Brand X's John Giblin formed the other half of a top-class rhythm section during these sessions, adding lyrical fretless bass. Giblin would later appear on Collins' first two solo albums and tour with Peter Gabriel.

'[Collins] and Martyn bonded quickly over a shared love of glassy jazz-funk and their furious, masculine heartaches,' writes Graeme Thompson in *Small Hours: The Long Night of John Martyn*. 'At the time, Collins was going through his own painful break-up. His marriage to his first wife, Andrea, had recently ended and he was licking his wounds, beginning the process of writing the painfully sad songs that would end up on his disarmingly direct debut album, *Face Value*. Misery loves company, particularly company that buys a round. The two men became playmates.'

Indeed, there's a clear emotional connection between *Grace and Danger* and *Face Value* – both men are writing about the break-up of their respective marriages. 'Save Some (For Me)' could almost be an outtake from *Face Value*, with Collins excelling on edgy drums and clear-as-a-bell backing vocals.

'I fell in love with John and his music during these sessions,' said Collins. 'He and I seem[ed] to musically hit it off.'

It was during this period that Phil first met Eric Clapton. Martyn had called Clapton looking to score drugs and was invited to contribute to *Grace and Danger*.

'It just didn't gel for some reason,' says producer Martin Levan. 'Lots of different egos floating about. I tried editing some bits to try to get something, but I couldn't.'

This unsuccessful session would mark the first of many with Collins and Clapton over the next ten years.

Grace and Danger, however, was not well received by Island Records. 'Chris Blackwell thought it was too miserable to release, which is very true,' Martyn said in an interview with John Neil Munro in 2004.

Finally made available in October 1980, the album was a modest commercial success, reaching number 54 in the UK charts. Martyn toured the UK and Italy for five weeks in October and November 1980 to promote his new album, taking Collins on drums and backing vocals, Max Middleton on keyboards, Jeff Allen on percussion and Alan Thomson on fretless bass.

1981

Skinningrove Bay, Playing For Time and Immunity

Skinningrove Bay is a solo album by saxophonist/flautist Jack Lancaster. Lancaster was a founder member of the British blues rock band Blodwyn Pig (1969 to 1972) with ex-Jethro Tull guitarist Mick Abrahams. A collaboration with keyboardist Robin Lumley in the studio band The Soul Searchers in 1975 led to two albums which both featured the contributions from future members of Lumley's band Brand X, John Goodsall, Percy Jones and Phil Collins: *The Rock Peter and the Wolf* (1975) and *Marscape* (1976).

'Skinningrove, North Yorkshire is the place I was born,' Lancaster told Aymeric Leroy c. 2002. 'The music was supposed to reflect the history of the coastal village. The intention was to include local folk music entwined with a rock feel. *Skinningrove Bay* was recorded for Acrobat Records, which paid for the sessions. It was never completely finished because I exceeded the budget. Robin [Lumley] and I mixed it anyway and then the shit hit the fan and Acrobat filed for bankruptcy. The tapes ended up in the hands of a suitably named company Shanghai Records, who then released it in all sorts of crappy tasteless forms taking advantage of the well-known guests involved in the recording. I have never received any payment for publishing or sales. I have been in touch with the owner of the company and for years, he has promised to pay up, but I have received nothing.'

The 'well-known' guests include Gary Moore, Rod Argent, Bernie Frost and Phil Collins, who is credited as vocalist on one song. *Skinningrove Bay* is a fine collection of slow, proggy songs with a folky feel. Collins sings tentatively but beautifully on 'Deep Green', which is based around shimmering electric piano, 10CC-style backing vocals, a fat saxophone solo and fretless bass.

Recording and release details for *Skinningrove Bay* are vague – the album was first released in 1981 but may well have been recorded much earlier.

Phil Collins also performs on three tracks on the album *Playing For Time* by ex-Flaming Youth bandmate keyboardist Brian Chatton. Chatton had worked with Pat Travers, John Miles and Meat Loaf in the 70s and 80s.

Chatton writes in his lively memoirs:

> I continued my friendship with Phil even after the flame of Flaming Youth fizzled out. In 1981, he agreed to play four songs on my first solo LP with

> RCA called *Playing for Time*. Shortly afterwards, he came around to my flat and, after discussing what he would play, we got a little buzzed and attempted to light a few A.G.E.'s (Anal Gas Emissions) for old time's sake — smoking my missus out of the room in disgust — and laughing our heads off at each resulting fireball. We decided we would go see the movie *The Omen* and, as the time was ticking by, I pointed to the door. Whilst we were grabbing our coats, Phil mentioned that he also had an album coming out. 'Just let me play you one of the songs from my new album. Okay?' he asked, almost as an afterthought. 'Yeah, all right mate,' I agreed, anxiously looking at my watch out of the corner of my eye. 'But you know it's getting late, and if we are going to make this movie on time….' 'We'll be fine, don't worry!' replied a very confident Phil. He sits down at the piano and with a flourish, begins to play the opening to the now iconic, 'In The Air Tonight'. I listened for about five or six seconds to the very slow, stark intro consisting of the words 'I can feel it, coming in the air tonight…' … pause… longer pause… 'Oh, Lord!' I grimaced, thinking to myself, 'He's not gone all religious on me now, has he? And surely he's not making this up because of what we'd been putting in the air tonight, is he?'

Collins plays on 'Comin' On Stronger', 'Thru' The Window' and 'You Got It Comin''. *Playing For Time* has been out of print for many years.

Chatton also notes that during his time with Pat Travers: 'I was busy writing my own material then and ended up recording two songs initially for Polygram. The line-up for these two songs was Pat [Travers], Nicko McBrain and Clog, Pat's [bass] guitarist. We also did another session using Phil Collins (as always for no charge), Pat and Gary Twigg.' This activity seems to date from c. 1976, so is outside the scope of this book. The tracks remain unreleased.

In this same period, Collins added percussion to two tracks from Rupert Hine's album *Immunity*. Hine, who died in 2020, was a well-respected record producer with a quirky low-key parallel career as a performer. British readers might remember the 1979 hit 'The Lone Ranger' by Quantum Jump – which Hine wrote and sang – as much as for his production credits on albums by Yvonne Elliman, Kevin Ayers, Anthony Phillips, Camel, Saga, The Waterboys, Tina Turner, Howard Jones, Chris De Burgh, The Fixx, Bob Geldof, Stevie Nicks, Rush, Suzanne Vega and others.

'Another Stranger' and 'Immunity' are dark and intriguing, even if the percussion could be by anyone.

Face Value

Personnel:
Phil Collins: vocals, drums, keyboards, percussion, acoustic guitar
Daryl Stuermer: guitars, banjo
Eric Clapton: guitar on 'If Leaving Me Is Easy'
Joe Partridge: slide guitar on 'The Roof Is Leaking'
John Giblin: bass guitar on 'In The Air Tonight', 'Thunder And Lightning', 'I'm Not Moving', 'Tomorrow Never Knows'
Alphonso Johnson: bass on 'This Must Be Love', 'Behind The Lines', 'Hand In Hand', 'I Missed Again', 'If Leaving Me Is Easy'
L. Shankar: violin on 'In The Air Tonight', 'Droned', 'I Missed Again', 'Tomorrow Never Knows'; tamboura and voice drums on 'Droned'
J. Peter Robinson: keyboards on 'Behind The Lines'
Stephen Bishop: background vocals on 'This Must Be Love'
Ronnie Scott: tenor saxophone on 'I Missed Again'
The EWF Horns: Don Myrick: tenor saxophone, alto saxophone; Louis Satterfield: trombone; Rahmlee Michael Davis and Michael Harris: trumpets, flugelhorn
Recorded June 1980–January 1981 at The Townhouse, London; Old Croft, Shalford, Surrey; The Village Recorder, Los Angeles.
Produced by Phil Collins and Hugh Padgham
Album release: 13 February 1981.
Highest chart placings: UK; 1, US: 7
Side one: 'In The Air Tonight', 'This Must Be Love', 'Behind The Lines', 'The Roof Is Leaking', 'Droned', 'Hand In Hand'
Side two: 'I Missed Again', 'You Know What I Mean', 'Thunder And Lightning', 'I'm Not Moving', 'If Leaving Me Is Easy', 'Tomorrow Never Knows', 'Over the Rainbow'

'In The Air Tonight' b/w 'The Roof Is Leaking'

Single release: 5 January 1981. Highest chart position: UK: 2; US: 19.

'I Missed Again' b/w 'I'm Not Moving'

Single release: 7 March 1981. Highest chart position: UK: 14; US: 19.

'If Leaving Me Is Easy' b/w 'In The Air Tonight', 'I Missed Again', 'If Leaving Me Is Easy (demo)'

UK single release: May 1981.
Highest chart position: 17.

> *Face Value* delights in confounding the familiar parameters of [Genesis'] style. Listening to this album is like meeting someone you thought you knew and disliked and discovering that they've got far more going for themselves than you ever imagined. *Face Value* confirms Collins as something of a musical cosmopolitan: a more suburban imagination would probably have selected one style and disciplined its repertoire to fit. Collins runs riot through a variety of settings, committing himself to the disparate moods and styles with genuine zeal.
> Allan Jones, *Melody Maker*, 1981

Face Value started with a series of parallel events moving together: Collins' marital problems, the Genesis band members' ability to record at home and the space for Collins to focus on some high-quality demos.

Once the *Duke* tour had concluded, Collins returned to his batch of confessional songs from the previous year. 'That summer of 1980,' he noted in his memoirs, 'I turn[ed] my attention back to the songs I wrote the year before. Time to put my recordings where my heart is.'

Genesis studio tech Geoff Callingham created a home recording set-up in Collins' former marital bedroom: an eight-track recorder, a Fender Rhodes piano, a Prophet-5 synthesizer and a Roland drum machine. He also hauled Collins' great-auntie Daisy's vintage 1820 Collard & Collard upright piano to his new home studio. The songs are very simple – usually just two or three chords and improvised vocal melodies and lyrics.

'Over a year,' Collins wrote later, 'these doodles of mine slowly take shape. But they are doodles. Nothing is really prepared or finished. Yet nonetheless, gradually, without me even noticing really, doodles become sketches become outlines become mini-portraits. Become songs.'

Eventually, he copied his batch of demos to cassette and, with his manager's support, played them to legendary Atlantic Records' boss, Ahmet Ertegun 'I hadn't really anticipated playing anything of mine to Ahmet. But I always had a tape in my car, so I could listen to the demos and come up with new ideas to add. Anyway, Ahmet listens to these demos and declares with emphatic enthusiasm, 'THIS IS A RECORD! Anything I can help you with, I will. But this has to be a record.'

Collins next turned to engineer and co-producer Hugh Padgham. 'A few months after I finished Peter [Gabriel]'s record, I was rung up by Tony Smith,' Padgham is quoted saying in *Genesis: Chapter and Verse*. 'Was I interested in working with Phil? 'Bloody hell, yes.' I drove down to meet Phil at his house. We played frisbee in the garden, listened to his demos and made a game plan from there. We both had the same kind of production ethic: to keep things really simple.'

'So we copy my eight-tracks onto sixteen-track,' Collins wrote in 2016, 'and throughout winter 1980/1981 we carry on overdubbing at Townhouse.'

Hugh Padgham: 'We used the bones from his demos and carried on working on those.'

Eric Clapton added guitar onto two tracks. His part on 'The Roof Is Leaking' was later replaced but can be heard on the 2016 reissue. The Earth, Wind and Fire horn section were overdubbed in Los Angeles.

The lead single and arguably Collins' most famous song, 'In The Air Tonight', was 'totally improvised.'

> One day, from out of the ether, I get together a nice chord sequence. Without even thinking about it, I soon have a working title based on the lyrics I've sung: 'In The Air Tonight'. It's 99.9 percent sung spontaneously, the words dreamt up from out of nowhere.

Originally the sparse drum machine was used throughout the song. Phil in *Playboy* in 1986:

> I resisted [drum machines] for a long time, but sometimes their insistence, the fact that they never change, makes them work in a way real drums don't. In a sense, it freed me. It changed the way I wrote. Also, the sounds you can create are almost infinite. The atmosphere on 'In The Air Tonight' is from the drum machine. So, yes, I love drum machines.

That famous drum break was added during overdub sessions at The Townhouse's 'stone room' – a live room faced in Cotswold stone that had been dug from the garden of Virgin's Manor Studios in Oxfordshire.

'The room was live, with a stone-slabbed floor,' engineer Mick Glossop told Howard Massey in *Behind The Glass, Volume One.* 'Given the context of the day, it was very live. If you hit a snare drum… it was incredible. We were contemplating changing the acoustics in there because we felt it was… uncontrollable. But it went on to become the vehicle for a classic drum sound.'

> You can control how much 'liveness' you want in the recording by closing heavy curtains to deaden the sound. And if you put the microphones in

> the top corners of the room, you can make the drums sound much more live. But for 'In The Air Tonight', we say, 'Let's try that sound we had with Pete…' What we actually end up with is nowhere as extreme as 'Intruder.' Even if you place the mics in the same place and try for the same sound, you'll always end up with a different animal. Different day, different result. As for that drum fill: people ask about it all the time. A landmark in percussion, in production, in ba-doom, ba-doom, ba-doom, ba-doom, doom-doom.

Collins told *Uncut*: 'I didn't think about the drum fill, I just did it that particular take and that's the one we used. We didn't sit there thinking, 'Oh boy, their mouths are going to be dropping when they hear this!' It was nothing like that.'

> But I soon realize that nobody has heard drums like this, as loud as this, and with that kind of sound. Beyond that, lyrically, too, the song has that something about it that nobody really understands. Not even me. Maybe because I'm not a songwriter — not yet, not really — it's outside the box of traditional songwriting. It's simple; it's ghostly, it's full of space, it's a *cri de cœur*. It should definitely not be a single.

'It will be on my gravestone,' Collins told Michael Hann in 2018. 'He came, he went, and in the middle, he did Da-Da, Da-Da, Da-Da.'

The buzzing guitar is by long-time Collins associate Daryl Stuermer, who recalled to *Uncut* magazine in 2008:

> My guitar part was done much later, in a studio in LA. I sat in the control room with Phil, and my amp was out in the studio, as loud as I could get it. I hit this chord, which Phil described as the sound of an electric razor, Rrrrzzzzz. People write me emails about that chord, asking what it is. The song's in the key of D minor, but the chord itself has no minor notes. It's a low A, and a D, and another A and a D. But it depends how you play it, it has to have that overdriven, distorted sound from the amp. It's a distant sound, but a distant powerful sound. It's a sound you imagine being deafeningly loud a mile away.

The song was remixed for a single release. More drums were added, which adds a recognisable backbeat. In the process, the song lost much of the tension. Nevertheless, 'In The Air Tonight' peaked at number two in the first week of February behind 'Woman' by John Lennon. Collins appeared on *Top Of The Pops* on 15 January, miming his vocals, sitting at a Prophet keyboard in a knitted tank-top, knees jiggling to the beat. He is twenty-nine years old and his world has just changed.

And herein starts the myth of the rogue paint pot. Despite its opaque lyrics, 'In The Air Tonight' is clearly a response to Collins' marital discord. And as the legend goes, he cheekily placed a pot of paint on top of his drum machine to make a sly dig at his wife for having an affair with a painter and decorator. Or, as Collins would have it, the pot was simply set décor.

> It has nothing to do with Andy going off with the decorator. That performance, and that paint pot, have come back to haunt me time and time again.

Collins might protest too much here – a similar paint pot can be seen during his performance of 'In The Air Tonight' at Drury Lane later that year.

The song has charted in the UK on four different occasions. On its original release in 1981, it peaked at number two. In 1988 a re-mix by Dutch DJ and producer Ben Liebrand got to number four – Liebrand adds some electronic percussion and reverb. In 2001, Collins' original formed the basis of Brooklyn rapper Lil Kim's 'In The Air Tonite' – this reached number 26 and was also released on the R&B/hip hop Phil Collins tribute album *Urban Renewal*. This includes a version of 'Sussudio' by Ol' Dirty Bastard and contributions by Brandy, Pharrell Williams, Montel Jordan, Dane Bowers and others. Finally, in 2007 the original mix of 'In The Air Tonight' was featured in a TV advert for Cadbury's Dairy Milk chocolate, notably featuring a drumming gorilla. The song was re-released and reached number fourteen.

> The haunting 'In The Air Tonight' is Phil Collins' first solo hit. Despite all the success he's had since, it remains the most famous work of his entire career. 'That's going to be on my headstone,' Collins said in 2013. 'He came. He wrote 'In The Air Tonight.' He. . . died.' The lyrics have been analyzed for decades and are the source of a persistent urban legend that Collins saw a man refuse to save another man from drowning, but the truth is significantly more boring. They simply came to Phil one day at his house while he was messing around with an early

> drum machine. The anger evident in the song is loosely directed at his ex-wife, but there's no grand story behind it. Collins swears he offered the song to Genesis, but the rest of the guys claim to have no memory of this. Whatever the truth, he released it on his own and it became a global sensation. Every few years, another soundtrack or commercial introduces it to a whole new audience.
> *Rolling Stone*, December 2013

The b-side is equally good: the stark, haunting, but optimistic 'The Roof Is Leaking' in which Collins takes the persona of a father wanting to protect his children. The acoustic slide guitar is credited to Joe Partridge, replacing a part originally recorded by Eric Clapton, who can be heard playing a very similar part on an alternative version released in 2016.

> Phil Collins is the first to admit that he wasn't a very good husband and father in the 1970s. It couldn't have been a huge shock when his wife left him, but the pain was nearly unbearable; she took both kids and even the dogs. The gut-wrenching 'The Roof Is Leaking' … is a sparse track, totally unlike anything the songwriter had done in his decade with Genesis. Few people could have imagined this material would kick-start one of the most successful pop careers of the decade.
> *Rolling Stone*, December 2013

Two other singles were lifted from the album in the first half of 1981: the punchy 'I Missed Again' and the sedate 'If Leaving Me Is Easy'.

'I Missed Again', originally titled 'I Miss You, Babe', is an explicit nod to Collins' 60s soul influences. Starting with a Motown drum fill, 'I Missed Again' is self-deprecating; the downbeat mood of the lyrics is lifted by The Phenix Horns. The silky tenor sax solo is by English jazz tenor saxophonist and jazz club owner Ronnie Scott. As Collins told *The Mail on Sunday*: 'This song was written with a large dose of humour, with a theme a little like the Basil Fawlty scene which goes something like, 'That was your life mate.' 'Do I get another chance?' 'No mate, that's it.''

'If Leaving Me Is Easy' is smooth, almost jazzy and utterly beautiful – but there is audible pain in Collins' crushingly honest vocal performance. Eric Clapton plays guitar, but with such restraint, you'd barely notice. As Collins told *The Mail on Sunday*: 'One of my favourite songs. It was so simple and yet said so much about how I felt at the time… the main chorus line being a real truism.' The chorus lyrics were the only words in place in Collins' original demo released in 2020. Here, at least, Clapton's exquisite guitar playing is present and correct.

The Isley Brothers recorded their own bittersweet version of 'If Leaving Me Is Easy' on their 1985 album *Masterpiece*, with strings and a very soulful lead vocal by O'Kelly Isley. It's worth a listen. Its inclusion of this recording on Phil Collins' *Plays Well With Others* box set suggests that Collins himself performs on this song – if so, he is uncredited.

The rest of the album contains many highlights. 'Behind The Lines' reworked from *Duke* with a funky bass line and horns. 'This Must Be Love' – the single that never was – and 'Thunder And Lightning' provide a hint of hope, as Collins told *The Mail on Sunday* on 28 March 2010: 'People generally consider my album *Face Value* as sad, but there are a number of songs on it that show a break in the clouds. 'This Must Be Love' is one.'

> Not all the songs I've written are doom and gloom. 'This Must Be Love' ('Happiness is something I never thought I'd feel again / but now I know / it's you that I've been looking for') and 'Thunder And Lightning' ('They say thunder / and they say lightning / it will never strike twice / but if that's true / then why can't you tell me / how come this feels so nice?') are the songs that move the personal narrative onward. These are the Jill songs, written post mid-1980.

'Droned' and 'Hand In Hand' are a pair of instrumentals. 'Droned' is short and atmospheric and features the violin, tamboura and voice skills of Lakshminarayana Shankar. It sounds a lot like Peter Gabriel, with whom Shankar has worked extensively. 'Hand In Hand' is a schizophrenic blend of Brand X jazz-funk and Motown horns.

'You Know What I Mean' is another piano ballad, exquisite and warm. 'I'm Not Moving' has an upbeat arrangement hiding a vicious message.

Face Value closes with two cover versions. 'Tomorrow Never Knows' and 'Over the Rainbow'. Collins' unexpected cover of the last track on The Beatles' 1966 masterpiece *Revolver* is a fine tribute, mixing Ringo's asynchronous drum pattern with John Giblin's octave-leaping bass and powerful, swirling 1980s keyboards. It's a triumph. The thirty-second *a capella* snippet of Judy Garland's most famous song was not listed on the original album. It seems appropriate and oddly affecting.

Just as *Face Value* was released, Phil was interviewed by Capital Radio's Nicky Horne. Much of the album was aired along with Phil's original demos of 'In The Air Tonight' (never heard since) and 'Please Don't Ask'.

Face Value entered the UK charts on 21 February 1981 for an initial run of forty-one weeks. It would return for long stretches throughout the decade, ultimately spending 270 weeks – over five years – in the British best-selling albums list during the 1980s. In the US, it would eventually sell over million copies: not bad for a low-key album recorded mostly in a bedroom.

'I didn't see it as making a record,' Collins said later. 'It wasn't cathartic, but it was obviously therapeutic.'

Collins' original demo of 'This Must Be Love' was included on the 2016 deluxe reissue of *Face Value* alongside three others used on other projects. This version of 'This Must Be Love' confirms the quality of Collins' original home recordings.

An otherwise unheard song, 'Please Don't Break My Heart' from the original batch of demos was made available as an mp3 download from Collins' website in 2011. This contains parts later reused in 'I'm Not Moving' and the Genesis song 'Me And Virgil'.

Glorious Fool

As *Face Value* was being released and with 'In The Air Tonight' riding high in the singles charts, Phil Collins returned to the Townhouse to produce a new album for John Martyn. Martyn used his touring band comprising Alan Thomson (bass), Danny Cummings (percussion) and Max Middleton (keyboards). Phil Collins provides drums, backing vocals and, on 'Don't You Go', piano.

> The blokey rock muso playing in a pub darts team with Martyn a year ago was now an internationally successful pop star. Little wonder, perhaps, that the drums on *Glorious Fool* are prominent to the point of intrusion. Who could blame Martyn for hoping that a little of that commercial fairy dust might flutter in his direction? Steve Sutherland's positive review in *Melody Maker* called the album a 'blatant bid for the long-deserved big time, emphatically more mainstream than its predecessors, and reminiscent of Collins' soulful solo efforts', all of which was correct. Graham Lock, in a scathing review for *NME*, heard only 'upmarket competence... the unruly maverick has become neat, tidy and polite. There is no drive, no depth to *Glorious Fool*; no grace or danger.' This also had the clear ring of truth.
>
> Graeme Thompson, *Small Hours: The Long Night of John Martyn,* 2020

'John at that time was slightly lost, very unorganised, and Phil stepped in with a lot of optimism,' engineer Nick Launay told Graeme Thompson. 'He had lists and a plan, whereas John's was completely a jazz approach. If we had to go back to fix something, even an hour later, he had already retuned his guitar to something else and couldn't remember what the previous tuning was. I think Phil sometimes was a little frustrated: 'How can you not remember what you played?' It was absolute chaos, but it didn't matter because it all sounded good. Recording vocals with him, I was just transfixed by his voice. I remember thinking it was like treacle and honey, just beautiful.'

Glorious Fool was released in September 1981, Martyn's first album for his new label, WEA. Martyn's bid for the mainstream charted for seven weeks in the UK, reaching number 25, his highest-charting album thus far.

Early in the sessions, Martyn was booked on the long-running and much-loved BBC music programme *The Old Grey Whistle Test.* He performed 'Sweet Little Mystery' and 'Lookin' On' with Phil Collins bashing the drums and singing backing vocals on 'Sweet Little Mystery'. These very fine performances, recorded on 10 January 1981, are available on the 2007 reissue of Martyn's *Grace and Danger* album.

Phil's First Solo Gig

Phil Collins stepped out tentatively as a solo artist. *Top Of The Pops* on 15 January 1981 was followed, six months later, by a mimed performance of 'In The Air Tonight' during the Una Canzone per L.A. Vostra Estate radio and television singing competition in Saint-Vincent, Italy on 27 June.

More importantly, Phil appeared in London on 11 and 12 September, singing two songs as part of a short series of benefit shows staged by the British Section of Amnesty International. This was the fourth in a long series of benefits starting in 1976.

Accompanying himself on a nine-foot Bechstein piano (with the paint pot duly in place), 'In The Air Tonight' starts hesitantly, but Collins' confidence builds and by its conclusion, he is singing brilliantly. It's 'a rare moment of chilling energy' according to Collins' biographer Ray Coleman.

Organiser and co-producer Martin Lewis requested 'Follow You Follow Me', but Collins performed 'The Roof Is Leaking' which he sang beautifully with effortless control. Guitarist Daryl Stuermer was at his side at this and pretty much every subsequent solo and group concert. Collins also joins the all-hands-on-deck finale of 'I Shall Be Released', bashing a tambourine.

A film version called *The Secret Policeman's Other Ball* includes 'In The Air Tonight' and 'I Shall Be Released' and footage of 'The Roof Is Leaking' can be viewed on YouTube.

All three songs can be heard on *The Secret Policeman's Other Ball – The Album*, released in March 1982. It's perhaps worth noting that the bass player in the house band for these concerts was Mo Foster, who would later work extensively with Phil Collins.

Abacab

Personnel:
Tony Banks: keyboards
Phil Collins: drums, vocals
Mike Rutherford: guitars, bass guitars
Additional musicians: The Phenix Horns on 'No Reply At All': Don Myrick: tenor saxophone, alto saxophone; Louis Satterfield: trombone; Rahmlee Michael Davis and Michael Harris: trumpets, flugelhorn. Arranged by Thomas Washington.
Recorded March–June 1981 at The Farm, Chiddingfold, Surrey.
Produced by Genesis and Hugh Padgham
Album release: 18 September 1981.
Highest chart placings: UK; 1, US: 7.
Side one: 'Abacab', 'No Reply At All', 'Me And Sarah Jane', 'Keep It Dark'
Side two: 'Dodo'/'Lurker', 'Who Dunnit?', 'Man On The Corner', 'Like It or Not', 'Another Record'

'Abacab' (single edit) b/w 'Another Record'

UK single release: 14 August 1981. Highest chart position: 9.

'No Reply At All' b/w 'Naminanu' / 'Dodo'

US single release: 9 September 1981. Highest chart position: 29.

'Keep It Dark' b/w 'Naminanu'

UK single release: 23 October 1981. Highest chart position: 33.

'Abacab' b/w 'Whodunnit?'

US single release: December 1981. Highest chart position: 26.

'Man On The Corner' b/w 'Submarine'

Single release: 5 March 1982. Highest chart position: UK: 41; US: 40.

> The only conscious decision we ever made [to be more commercial] was in about 1981, when we did the album *Abacab*. We thought we'd make it a little bit more concise. We always did long and short songs, we just got better at the short ones.
> Tony Banks, *Classic Pop*, August 2018

> Genesis prove with this album that they will not allow the grass to grow under their highly-revered feet. The band are workaholics and hard slog has produced numbers like the title track, which is probably one of the best things they have ever done – raunchy, lively stuff showing Collins at his most streetwise and all three at their most inventive.
> Cathi Wheatley, *Sounds*, September 1981

If *Duke* was the pivot of the move from art rock to the drive towards commerciality, by the time of *Abacab* – the first Genesis album started after the initial success of *Face Value* – Collins, Banks and Rutherford were unwilling to compromise. The introduction of the Earth, Wind and Fire horn section and the silliness of 'Who Dunnit?' are proof of a band that wanted to experiment. They lost fans along the way but gained many, many more.

As Robin Platts writes, 'In 1981 Genesis abandoned much of their trademark sound and more or less started from scratch. For better or worse, *Abacab* was the reinvention of Genesis.'

The album was written collectively and recorded at their own newly-built studios, The Farm in Chiddingfold, Surrey, in spring 1981.

'There was a big difference between working in our studio and going away to do it, and feeling that you had to keep to a schedule.' Collins told Hugh Fielder of *Sounds* in September 1981. 'If something wasn't happening, we would just stop and do something else. Before, we'd have felt obliged to keep on trying to get it right. There are a couple of songs that would have died under the old method.'

The achievements of *Face Value* also changed the band's approach. 'During the writing of *Abacab,* news slowly filters through of *Face Value*'s unexpected success' Collins recalled. 'This makes things a little awkward. I'll come in all bubbly and genuinely gobsmacked: 'My God, 'In The Air Tonight' has reached number one in Holland!' Not only that, it's becoming a smash all over the world. *Face Value* keeps selling and selling.'

'We were in the early stages of writing *Abacab* when 'In The Air Tonight' was released,' Mike Rutherford explains in his memoirs. 'Phil came in the next morning and we all looked at each other: 'That's not bad, is it?' We were all quite surprised, Phil included.' And as Tony Banks pithily says in the 2014 BBC documentary *Genesis: Together and Apart*: 'We wanted Phil to do well. Just not that well.'

'The trio resolved to make the music on *Abacab* different from anything they had recorded before', writes Steve Aldous in *The Songs of Genesis* (2020). 'They would throw out any song in which they felt they were repeating themselves. There would be no extensive keyboard solos. The drums would be brought up in the mix. They would simplify the song format and keep the arrangements sparse.'

'[Phil] gained confidence as a writer, clearly,' Tony Smith told Ray Coleman. 'And within the group, it became more of an equal partnership. It wasn't until he did his own record that he realised that Tony and Mike, when they wrote the lyrics, did not write as singers. So they would put them in the wrong key, or they'd write the lyric before he'd sung it. And, of course, it was difficult to sing.'

> The creative revelation of performing his own material was very important to the evolution of Phil Collins. 'I was always having to sing songs about things I know nothing about,' he told me. 'And I'm being our worst critic here. 'All In A Mouse's Night' [from *Wind & Wuthering*, lyrics by Tony Banks] was a song I had to sing. Tony and Mike were great at writing 'ideas songs'. But while it's great to write them, to sing them and get behind them, putting emotion into a song about a mouse and a bit of bread is very hard. And I started to get very frustrated about that.'
>
> Ray Coleman, *Phil Collins The Definitive Biography*, 1997

As Collins wrote more of his own lyrics, which naturally better suited his delivery style, his singing became more confident. His developing compositional skills and vocal style influenced Genesis noticeably after 1981 – he would write the lyrics for the hit singles 'No Reply At All', 'Man On The Corner', 'Paperlate', 'Mama', 'That's All', 'Taking It All Too Hard', 'Invisible Touch', 'Tonight, Tonight, Tonight' and 'In Too Deep' as well as all five singles taken from *We Can't Dance*.

For *Abacab* Genesis recruited Hugh Padgham as co-producer and engineer. As David Hentschel told Steve Aldous: 'Phil's solo success and the sound he was getting with Hugh were surely a big influence, not only on my position but very obviously on the future of Genesis as well.'

Padgham brought a bright eighties sound to *Abacab*. His huge drum sound necessitated a simpler approach to the musical texture and aural production.

> Hugh and I had worked together on Gabriel's albums and we'd worked together on my things. Because of him, we ended up with a monster drum sound. It took up so much space that there was less room for other musical material. This is one of the reasons why musically and texturally, our music became a little sparser. With that big drum sound, there was a little less room for everything else.
> Phil Collins quoted in *Genesis: Peter Gabriel, Phil Collins & Beyond*, 1984

Whilst there were nods to Genesis' arty past and prog pedigree on *Abacab* with songs such as 'Dodo', 'Lurker' and the middle parts of 'Abacab' and 'Me And Sarah Jane', the inclusion of 'Who Dunnit?' and the horn-laden 'No Reply At All' would horrify many older fans. The single 'Paperlate', recorded in these sessions, is as far from 'The Battle of Epping Forest' as one band could travel. Three of the songs that hark back most obviously to their earlier sound were sidetracked as b-sides.

'In retrospect, *Abacab* was a transition period,' Collins told Philip Kamin and Peter Goddard in 1984. 'At the time, it was the best thing we were doing. As all these new albums are, though. In each new album, we are going to try to do different things.'

Looking back, *Abacab* was a bold step. The band was booed in Europe when they played some of their new songs in concert, but in the US, they leapt up a couple of leagues in the popularity stakes: 'Misunderstanding' had been a top twenty hit single there the previous summer, so the band's desire to match that success in the same market would have been considerable. Both 'Abacab' and 'No Reply At All' would creep into the *Billboard* top thirty, so the pop/prog strategy was starting to bear fruit.

The Phil Collins effect was kicking in. Genesis' audience were diversifying and women were appearing in the audiences at gigs in greater numbers.

> Under [Collins'] increased influence, Genesis's quasi-symphonic, allegorical bombast gave way to leaner, more tuneful, trickily syncopated rock that has reversed the group's sagging commercial fortunes.
> Stephen Holden, *New York Times*, April 1985

Genesis' reinvention as a pop version of a progressive rock band was followed by the likes of Yes and Rush, who condensed the complexity and layering of prog into shorter, more commercial songs such as 'New World Man' (1982) and 'Owner Of A Lonely Heart' (1983), both sizable hit singles. Old-school fans were critical of the changes in all three of these bands that had roots in the 1970s but pressed for significant change in the early 1980s.

> By *Abacab* I felt much more involved in the writing and the production was sounding even better. Both sides of my career were quite happily running in parallel.
> Phil Collins, *Genesis: Chapter and Verse* (2007)

Abacab opens with the blast of the seven-minute title track. This was edited for a single release and made available in the UK four weeks ahead of the album. British listeners immediately embraced their new sound, pushing the track to number nine for Genesis' third top ten single in their home country. 'Abacab' would develop into a monster live, stretching to twelve minutes or more. The version from Wembley Stadium, 4 July 1987, is seriously impressive. 'No Reply At All' is an upbeat track, a very definite move towards the mainstream, with its simple chorus, powerful bridge and parping horn section. Mike Rutherford's bubbling prog-soul bassline is wonderful. 'No Reply At All' was released as a single in the US in preference to 'Abacab'.

Banks' 'Me And Sarah Jane' is closer to the older Genesis sound, with rippling keyboards and a tinkling drum machine. A proggy section from 3:35 includes a beautiful swirling synth sound over sliding bass notes.

Tony Banks: 'I poured all this flowery stuff into one song and reminded myself to keep it simple on the rest of the album. It's probably my last Genesis song that had those chord changes.'

Side one closes with 'Keep It Dark' which is based on a repeating two-bar drum sample, and has falsetto vocals and alarming instrumental interludes. Steve Aldous cites this song as an example of Genesis achieving 'maximum impact with the minimum of fuss and in so doing created something very different from any other band, while remaining uniquely Genesis'. 'Keep It Dark' was released as the album's second single in the UK but reached only number thirty-three.

'Dodo' and 'Lurker' are a powerful, aggressive one-two of stirring, dynamic writing and performance. One ongoing discussion among

Genesis fans is whether these two tracks were part of a longer 'Dodo Suite'. Tony Banks: 'Originally, we had four tracks which we joined together of which these are the first two and the other two we decided to shelve because they weren't very strong and so in a way we consider them as separate songs. In fact, there is a definite breakpoint and then you are into a different kind of feel.'

Certainly, the track 'Submarine', released as the b-side of 'Man On The Corner', opens with an identical drum pattern to the (rapid) fade-out of 'Lurker'. The other component of this potential suite is 'Naminanu', which was released as the b-side of 'No Reply At All' along with an edit of 'Dodo'. 'Submarine' echoes the work of Pink Floyd, down to replicating Nick Mason's lazy tom-tom fills. 'Naimanu' is a jazzy semi-instrumental in the Weather Report vein and is truly wonderful.

Originally labouring under the working title 'Weird Synth', 'Who Dunnit?' is a throwaway joke based on an annoyingly repetitive melody and lyric. It's difficult to understand its inclusion at the expense of the elegant 'You Might Recall', the dreamy 'Submarine' or the dynamic 'Naminanu'. But the manic 'Who Dunnit?', like it or not, represented a statement of intent. 'Ian Dury gone electronic', as Cathi Wheatley would have it in *Sounds*.

'Man On The Corner' is the closest song on *Abacab* to echo Phil Collins' work on *Face Value*, especially with its simple keyboard pads, the Roland TR-808 drum machine and the sincere, fully-committed lead vocal.

> My favourite track is 'Man On The Corner,' which is the only song credited solely to Collins, a moving ballad with a pretty synthesized melody plus a riveting drum machine in the background. Though it could easily come off any of Phil's solo albums because the themes of loneliness, paranoia and alienation are overly familiar to Genesis, it evokes the band's hopeful humanism. 'Man On The Corner' profoundly equates a relationship with a solitary figure (a bum, perhaps a poor homeless person?), 'that lonely Man On The Corner' who just stands around.
>
> Patrick Bateman, the central character of Bret Easton Ellis' 1991 novel *American Psycho.*

'Like It or Not' is an almost-lost gem, with glorious vocal harmonies and a brilliant lead vocal. Less successful is the closing 'Another Record' which uses material originally written during the *Duke* sessions and incessantly repeats the 'In The Air Tonight' drum fill. By this time, older Genesis fans may well have taken Collins' advice and 'put another record on'.

Abacab – three quarters or more of a really great album – was a big hit: another UK number one and top ten in the US The 2007 remix adds a warmth that was perhaps lacking in 1981.

With the title track originally running at fifteen minutes and five songs recorded but unused, Genesis had recorded enough music for a double album. Three of these unused tracks were peeled off as Genesis' second E.P.

3 x 3

Personnel:
Tony Banks: keyboards
Phil Collins: drums, vocals
Mike Rutherford: guitars, bass guitars
Additional musicians: The EWF Horns on 'Paperlate': Don Myrick: tenor saxophone, alto saxophone; Louis Satterfield: trombone; Rahmlee Michael Davis and Michael Harris: trumpets, flugelhorn
Recorded May–June 1981 at The Farm, Chiddingfold, Surrey.
Produced by Genesis.
EP release: 12 May 1982.
Highest chart placings: UK; 10; US: 32.
Side one: 'Paperlate', 'You Might Recall', Side two: 'Me And Virgil'

The E.P. *3 x 3* collects three unheard songs from the *Abacab* sessions. Another top ten hit in the UK, the catchy lead-off track 'Paperlate', which riffs from a line in 'Dancing with the Moonlit Knight' (''Paper late!' cried a voice in the crowd'), combines sixties soul and British prog and is not so far from Collins' 'I Missed Again'. Genesis appeared on *Top Of The Pops* on 27 May 1982 with a horn section that is patently not from the South Side of Chicago.

'You Might Recall' is a strong song with a romantic undertone and jangly jazz guitar. It seems a shame that this was not included on *Abacab* instead of 'Who Dunnit'. The six-minute 'Me And Virgil' could be from *And Then There Were Three* or *Duke*. Its psychedelic guitar solo sounds a lot like The Band, whose 1969 song 'The Night They Drove Old Dixie Down' opens with the line 'Virgil Kane is the name / And I served on the Danville train'.

The E.P.'s title is a nod to The Rolling Stones' 1964 E.P. *5 x 5* and the cover artwork is a homage to the design of The Beatles' 1963 *Twist and*

Shout E.P. In the US, 'Paperlate' and 'You Might Recall' were released as a regular 7" single.

Abacab Tour

The three-month *Abacab* tour commenced in Barcelona on 25 September 1981, progressing through Spain, France, the Netherlands, Germany, Belgium and Switzerland. The setlist generally comprised 'Behind The Lines', 'Duchess', 'The Lamb Lies Down On Broadway', 'Dodo/Lurker', 'Abacab', 'Misunderstanding', 'Man On The Corner', 'Who Dunnit?', 'No Reply At All', 'Firth Of Fifth', 'Me And Sarah Jane', In The Cage (Medley – 'The Cinema Show' – 'Colony Of The Slippermen' – 'Afterglow'), 'Turn It On Again', 'Dance On A Volcano', 'Drum Duet' and 'Los Endos', with 'I Know What I Like (In My Wardrobe)' as the encore.

Performing three-quarters of *Abacab* in the first half of the set was not universally popular. Infamously, the band's performances of several new songs were booed during the 3 October concert at the Groenoordhal in Leiden. Phil had strong words with the audience after 'Who Dunnit?' delivered in a semi-serious accent Redneck accent: 'You guys are gonna have a talk with me, boy. I don't wanna create no bad feeling here, boy, but if you don't like the new music you'd better get the hell out of here. Alright, alright. Just to make it all worthwhile for you people who like the old shit, we'll play some of the old music. This is one called 'Firth Of Fifth'…' And later, evidently only half-joking: 'Now that we've cheered everybody up, we'll play another new song now. Anyone who doesn't like it can come and meet me afterwards and I'll fuckin' kick the shit out them.'

Genesis performed across the US and Canada from mid-November through to mid-December. Their shows at the Savoy Theatre, New York City and Nassau Coliseum, Uniondale on 28 and 29 November were recorded and filmed. 'Misunderstanding' from the New York show along with 'Turn It On Again', 'Behind The Lines', 'Duchess' and 'Me And Sarah Jane' from Nassau, have been released on the album *Three Sides Live*. Two further songs from New York were later included on *Archive #2*: 'No Reply At All' and 'Man On The Corner'. 'Firth Of Fifth' from Nassau appeared on both a fan-club flexi-disc and the 12" single of 'That's All' in 1983. Video footage of these two shows were released as the concert film *Three Sides Live* in mid-1982.

Six concerts in the UK just before Christmas wrapped up activities for 1981. Recordings of the band's performance at the recently opened

Birmingham International Arena, located within the National Exhibition Centre, on 23 December 1981 provide recordings of 'Dodo / Lurker', 'Abacab', and 'In The Cage – The Cinema Show – Colony Of The Slippermen – Afterglow' as the balance of the forthcoming *Three Sides Live*.

1982

Disparate Session Work 1: Robert Plant

In 1982, Phil Collins worked on a new solo albums by Led Zeppelin's Robert Plant.

'Back home at Old Croft [in spring 1982], the phone rings,' Collins wrote in his memoirs. ''Hi, Phil. It's Robert Plant.' Despite my being a fan of Plant and Led Zeppelin from way back when, Robert and I have never met. He sends me a bunch of demos [and] I spend a couple of weeks at Rockfield Studios in Wales. We have lots of laughs between recording. Here are a great bunch of guys, and I'm in a band again, albeit for a short while.'

Although Collins writes that sessions took place in spring, the album's release date of June 1982 most likely pushed the dates to the very beginning of the year. Collins was on tour with Genesis from September to December 1981.

> I had always been part of a band, so I didn't know about autonomy, about democracy of the mind. Now I had to put my shoulders back and get into gear, and Phil was really instrumental in helping me shape my approach. The great thing at first was his humour and his charm, but what really inspired me was his energy and ability. He only had those four or five days available, but he would turn up and drive the sessions. He was the first guy back to the control room to listen to the playback to see if we were interpreting those songs in the most appropriate way.
> Robert Plant, *Plays Well With Others* sleeve notes, 2018

Collins plays on six of the eight tracks. The strutting 'Burning Down One Side' has a sub-Stones riff, with Phil keeping it simple. 'Moonlight In Samosa' is a mid-tempo crooner. It's drenched in reverb but unlike anything Plant had attempted previously. 'Pledge Pin' threatens to come off as a facsimile of The Police, but is sweetened by Raphael 'Baker Street' Ravenscroft's smooth saxophone. Collins' tempo-pushing drumming is excellent. The bluesy 'Worse Than Detroit' is reminiscent of the poppier moments of Led Zeppelin's output, whereas 'Fat Lip' is keyboard-heavy 80s lounge rock. The closing 'Mystery Title' is a shuffle with some loud drumming. Phil Collins is very much 'just one of the band' here. It's guitarist and co-writer Robbie Blunt who deserves the bouquets.

'Burning Down One Side,' the leadoff track, is a dead-on-target hit — a neck-wringing riff spiced with effortlessly atmospheric guitar leads — while the charming 'Fat Lip,' a bluesy riff located at the other end of the emotional spectrum, could almost give laid-back a good name again. Elsewhere, Plant trots out his trademark bellow for 'Slow Dancer' and the aforementioned 'Mystery Title,' and enlists the high, reedy tones of saxophonist Raphael Ravenscroft (noted for his work on the Gerry Rafferty hit, 'Baker Street') for the slightly unfocused 'Pledge Pin.' There are longueurs: 'Moonlight In Samosa,' for instance, is sort of like 'Stairway To Heaven' without the sonic liftoff, and 'Like I've Never Been Gone' ('I see the sunlight in your eyeeeeeeeeee …') is just sort of stupid. But when the good stuff on an album cuts all the other cock-rock competition in sight, only a curmudgeon would complain.
Kurt Loder, *Rolling Stone*, 16 August 1982

Pictures At Eleven entered the UK charts at number two the week after its release. The 2007 re-issue includes two bonus tracks, both featuring Phil Collins. 'Far Post', despite its jangling piano, was perhaps too similar to 'Pledge Pin' to have found a place on *Pictures At Eleven*. It was issued as the b-side to Plant's 1983 single 'Big Log'. Collins' tight drumming moves the song at a clip. The excellent live take of 'Like I've Never Been Gone' was recorded in Houston in September 1983, originally broadcast on King Biscuit Flower Hour in 1984.

Disparate Session Work 2. Frida

Abba had matured significantly since their success with 'Waterloo' at the 1974 Eurovision Song Content. Their final top three single in the UK had been the downbeat 'One Of Us' at the end of 1981. With the band on hiatus before recording sessions in August 1982, Frida took the opportunity to record her first English language solo album. It is coloured by her collapsed marriage to Benny Andersson. They had wed in 1978 after a ten-year relationship but by early 1981 had filed for divorce.

Frida had heard *Face Value* the previous summer, and, one assumes, the end-of-a-relationship themes that run through the album chimed with her. Collins wrote later.

Anni-Frid Lyngstad visits me at The Farm. She's been going through a divorce, too. With her personal life splintering she wants to make a solo album. I get the impression that she wants to stretch and be her own

> woman. She doesn't reveal much of this during our meeting at The Farm, only that she has chosen me to help her realize her goal. She's seemingly listened to *Face Value* incessantly, so she believes I understand and can relate to what she's going through. I tell her I can.

'I remember Phil ringing up one day,' engineer Hugh Padgham told Abba's biographer Carl Magnus Palm. ''You'll never guess who called and wants me to do an album – Frida from Abba!' Of course, Abba were still a big deal at the time.'

Six weeks of sessions at Polar Studios in Stockholm started in mid-February 1982. Martyn Ford's strings were added later at George Martin's Air Studios in London. Collins brought his regular solo band: Daryl Stuermer, Mo Foster and Peter Robinson along with engineer Padgham. This, inevitably, gives much of *Something's Going On* a distinctive Phil Collins sound.

Frida had listened to hundreds of submissions from British songwriters such as Chris Difford and Glen Tilbrook of Squeeze, Joe Jackson, Elvis Costello and Phil Lynott of Thin Lizzy.

'Sitting together at the studio,' Collins recalled, 'Frida and I choose the songs, but she has certain pre-booked numbers that preclude any argument. Abba's management put out a worldwide call for compositions and, from the hundreds of responses, an eclectic selection has been assembled. I've thrown in one by my pal Stephen Bishop, and she's chosen a Bryan Ferry number; a Giorgio Moroder co-write that appeared on a Donna Summer album the previous year; a Dorothy Parker poem set to music by the guy who would go on to found Roxette; a song that was the British entry for the 1980 Eurovision Song Contest; and a rework of my *Face Value* track 'You Know What I Mean.' Talk about a smörgåsbord.'

'I was expecting slightly more from her, to be honest,' says Hugh Padgham. 'She kind of let us do what we wanted to do on the music and then she just came and sang on the top of it, at the end of the day. The situation was probably much more intimidating for her than we realised.'

Perhaps inevitably, the album is an uneasy blend of Collins' roots in prog, his taste for American soul music and Frida wanting to rock a little – she had cited Pat Benatar as her starting point for the album. Ironically, perhaps the most successful song on the album is 'You Know What I Mean' from *Face Value,* with a softer, more wistful production. The drum-laden title track, written by Russ Ballard, was a global hit single entering the top five in several European countries and in

Australia, as well as number thirteen in the US Collins and Frida duet on the lightweight 'Here We'll Stay'.

The album was released in September 1982 and topped the charts in Belgium and Switzerland. It was a top five hit in Australia, Austria, France, Germany, the Netherlands, Norway, South Africa and Sweden amongst others, selling a respectable 1.5 million copies worldwide.

At least one song, 'Shot Down In Action,' remains unreleased. Collins completists need to track down the single version of 'Here We'll Stay', which includes re-recorded vocals by Frida.

> She was ever so nice. She thought I was a kindred spirit as she was going through this painful divorce, and she liked *Face Value* and she thought I'd understand her. That whole *Something's Going On* album is great.
> Phil Collins, *Classic Rock*, 2017

As a coda, Collins was approached in early 1984 to produce Frida's next solo album. By then, he was committed to a US tour with Genesis and sessions with Eric Clapton in Monserrat.

Disparate Session Work 3: Gary Brooker, Rupert Hine, Ralph McTell, Marti Webb

Clapton's keyboard player between late 1979 and late 1982 was ex-Procol Harum writer and pianist Gary Brooker. Phil Collins plays drums on the title track of Brooker's solo album *Lead Me to the Water*, released in March 1982. Brooker ran his own country pub at the time, close to Phil Collins' house. Other notable local George Harrison also appears on the album (although not with Collins) as does Eric Clapton, with whom Brooker had recorded a different, still unreleased, version of 'Lead Me To The Water' in 1980.

'Lead Me To The Water' is a tired reggae.

Collins worked again with Rupert Hine during this period, drumming and adding percussion to 'Innocents In Paradise' from Hine's second solo album *Waving Not Drowning*. Collins also appeared on stage with Hines at least once, adding spontaneous maracas, vibraslap and tambourine to a performance of 'The Set Up' recorded on 9 March 1982 for the Swedish TV show *Måndagsbörsen* (*The Monday Stock Exchange*). The programme was recorded in Stockholm and broadcast on Monday nights between 1979 and 1984. Collins looks very sheepish but was perhaps glad for the distraction from the concurrent sessions for Frida.

Phil's connection to John Martyn led to a session with renowned folkie Ralph McTell.

'My brother Bruce was managing John Martyn at the time,' McTell writes on his website. 'They had been working with a wonderful producer called Martin Levan. Martin arguably produced two of John's greatest albums at this time, *Grace and Danger* and *One World*. Bruce suggested Martin Levan and I try to work together. The two of us hit it off immediately. Martin had a quiet approach but was very strong and creatively one of the best guys ever behind the glass. We began working at his preferred studio in Willesden and later at Air London. He encouraged me to play solo for much of the sessions and as my trust grew in our mutual understanding, introduced various musicians I would never have thought of approaching. Most notably, Phil Collins. Phil was wonderful, very self-effacing and a little unsure of what he called 'folk stuff' nevertheless, he played with that marvellous slightly easy swing on the beat and the two tracks he played on really benefit from his approach.'

Both 'Cold on the Stones' and 'Song for Martin' are available on McTell's *Water of Dreams.* John Giblin's unmistakable bass playing underpins these songs, and master session guitarist Phil Palmer also contributes.

Marti Webb's album *Not That Kind Of Girl* was recorded between November 1981 and June 1982, and released in February 1983. Webb had some chart success in the early 1980s, notably the top three hit 'Take That Look Off Your Face', but was perhaps better known as a stage actor in West End musicals such as *Half a Sixpence*, *Godspell* and *Evita*. She was Nancy in both the first UK tour and the 1967 London revival of *Oliver!*, a few years after Phil Collins played the Artful Dodger in the same show. *Not That Kind Of Girl* was co-written and produced by David Hentschel – co-producer of four albums for Genesis between 1976 and 1980. Phil Collins unmistakably drums on the tracks 'No Problem' and 'Seven Outside Mr Chows' – the latter sounds like an early version of 'Home By The Sea'.

Princes Trust Rock Gala 1982

The first of several benefit concerts for The Prince's Trust was held at the Dominion Theatre in London on 7 July 1982. These were designed as one-off events with a 'house band' of famous musicians providing backing for different singers and also singing songs of their own.

In 1982, the band comprised Pete Townshend, Gary Brooker, Midge Ure and a formidable rhythm section of Phil Collins and Mick Karn. They performed 'No Regrets' (sung by Ure), 'Let My Love Open The Door' and 'Split Skirts' (sung by Townshend), and 'Whiter Shade Of Pale' (sung by Brooker) and also backed Ian Anderson ('Jack In The Green' and 'Pussy Willow'), Joan Armatrading ('Give Me Love'), Robert Plant (a terrific 'Worse Than Detroit', from *Pictures At Eleven*) and a rare live performance by Kate Bush, singing 'Wedding List'. Phil Collins performed a solo piano version of 'In The Air Tonight', yet again.

The entire company provided a marvellous finale of 'I Want To Take You Higher', originally by Sly and the Family Stone.

Three Sides Live

Personnel:
Tony Banks: keyboards
Phil Collins: drums, vocals
Mike Rutherford: guitars, bass guitars
Additional musicians (1976): Steve Hackett: guitar and Bill Bruford: drums
Additional musicians (1978-1981): Daryl Stuermer: guitar, bass and Chester Thompson: drums, percussion
Recorded live at the Apollo Theatre, Glasgow, 8 July 1976 ('It / Watcher Of The Skies'), Knebworth Festival, 24 June 1978 ('Fountain Of Salmacis'), Theatre Royal, Drury Lane, London, 5 May 1980 ('One For The Vine'), Lyceum Theatre, London, 7 May 1980 ('Follow You Follow Me'), the Savoy, New York City, 28 November 1981 ('Misunderstanding'), Nassau Coliseum, Uniondale, New York, 29 November 1981 ('Turn It On Again', 'Behind The Lines', 'Duchess', 'Me And Sarah Jane'), National Exhibition Centre, Birmingham, 23 December 1981 ('Dodo / Lurker', 'Abacab', 'In The Cage – 'The Cinema Show' – 'Colony Of The Slippermen' – 'Afterglow').
Produced by Genesis.
Album release: 4 June 1982.
Highest chart placings: UK; 2; US: 10.
Side one: 'Turn It On Again', 'Dodo' / 'Lurker', 'Abacab'
Side two: 'Behind The Lines', 'Duchess', 'Me & Sarah Jane', 'Follow You Follow Me'
Side three: 'Misunderstanding', In The Cage – 'The Cinema Show' – 'Colony Of The Slippermen' – 'Afterglow'
Side four: 'One For The Vine', 'Fountain Of Salmacis', 'It' / 'Watcher Of The Skies'
Side four (original North American edition): 'Paperlate' , 'You Might Recall', 'Me And Virgil', 'Evidence Of Autumn', 'Open Door'

Genesis' third live album includes in-concert performances of songs from *Wind & Wuthering*, *And Then There Were Three*, *Duke*, and *Abacab*. Of the 1981 recordings, only the 'In The Cage' medley represent pre-1976 Genesis. 'The Fountain Of Salmacis' and a medley of 'It' and 'Watcher Of The Skies' date from shows in 1976 and 1978 and were dropped for the North American release in preference to the tracks from *3 x 3* and some b-sides.

Genesis were, by now, hugely popular as an albums band. *Three Sides Live* reached an impressive number two in the UK and entered the top ten in the US, their second to do so.

A concert film of the same name was released in June 1982, directed by Stuart Orme. This features live performances of twelve songs from the Savoy, New York City and Nassau Coliseum, Uniondale, New York, on 28 and 29 November 1981. Some of these were remixed into 5.1 audio for the 2009 DVD along with undated performances of 'One For The Vine', 'Fountain Of Salmacis' (both presumably from the same sources as the original album) and 'Follow You Follow Me'.

Genesis toured for eight weeks to support the album: forty-five dates in the US, Canada, Europe and the UK. The set-list generally included 'Dance On A Volcano', 'Behind The Lines', 'Follow You Follow Me', 'Dodo/Lurker', 'Abacab', a crowd-pleasing final outing of 'Supper's Ready' 'Misunderstanding', 'Man On The Corner', 'Who Dunnit?', a medley of 'In The Cage' with excerpts from 'The Cinema Show', 'Riding The Scree' and 'Raven', 'Afterglow', 'Turn It On Again' and 'Los Endos' with the opening drum duet. The encore comprised 'The Lamb Lies Down On Broadway' and 'Watcher Of The Skies'.

The tour ended with three nights at the famed Hammersmith Odeon, Monday to Wednesday, 27-29 September.

Six Of The Best

During Genesis' Shepton Mallet show on 19 September, Peter Gabriel quietly joined the crowd to watch the performance of 'Supper's Ready', then slipped away. This presaged the on-stage reunion of Gabriel with the then-current five-man Genesis line-up on a rainy day in Buckinghamshire on Saturday, 2 October 1982.

Gabriel's ex-bandmates agreed to the one-off concert to ease financial pressure on his World of Music, Arts and Dance (Womad) organisation: their first world music festival earlier in 1982 had suffered a large loss.

'Having tried for seven years to get away from the image of being ex-Genesis, there's obviously a certain amount of [trepidation] stepping back,' Gabriel told the *NME* in 1982. 'I don't think they would choose at this point to work with me or, or I with them. It's very generous of them [to offer to help], and I'm very grateful.'

Sixty thousand fans attended Six Of The Best, as the concert was billed, at the National Bowl in Milton Keynes, with support from John Martyn, The Blues Band and Talk Talk.

For £9, patient and wet attendees enjoyed a well-balanced set of 1970-1975 highlights. 'Some of you may be wondering what we're doing here,' announced Gabriel from the stage. 'But actually, this is a sequence from a previous event by the name of Womad... a great event that lost a pile of money. But I'm very lucky to have a group of people [here] who support these ideals, so in return for your cash, we'll give you what we think you will like from this combination.'

The set included 'Back In N.Y.C.', the opening of 'Dancing With The Moonlit Knight', 'Carpet Crawlers', 'Firth Of Fifth', 'The Musical Box', 'The Lamb Lies Down On Broadway', 'Fly on a Windshield', 'Broadway Melody Of 1974', 'In The Cage' and 'Supper's Ready'. Gabriel's biggest solo hit to date 'Solsbury Hill' was performed by Genesis for the only time, and Gabriel sat behind Collins' drum kit for 'Turn It On Again'. Steve Hackett, flying in late from South America, joined the band for the encores of 'I Know What I Like (In Your Wardrobe)' and 'The Knife'. Collins:

> As reunions go, it's an odd one, but it's for a good cause — Peter had creditors threatening his life. As he later said, 'When the shit hit the fan, people identified me as the only fat cat worth jumping on, so I got the aggro, a lot of flak, nasty calls.' Still a band of brothers seven years after his departure, we all gladly pitch in to help, and the Bowl is packed with 47,000 fans for this once-in-a-lifetime gig. The incessant rain does its best to ruin the day. We've only had time for a couple of afternoon rehearsals during Genesis' recent gigs at Hammersmith Odeon, the song selection necessarily draws mainly from the Peter era, and the whole idea feels better on paper than it does in practice. Overall, though, the fans are pleased, and so are the critics. More importantly, we've helped stop our mate being jailed, or worse, and helped Womad live to fight another festival.

As photographer Robert Ellis recalled to *The Guardian* in 2012:

> It was a terrible show. An awful show. They pulled it off only because they wanted to, but in terms of a performance, it was hardly their finest hour.

> There are a couple of bootlegs going around, and I wouldn't urge anyone to go and listen to them because they're really not very good. If you heard those bootlegs, you'd be forced to agree with what I'm saying.

Recordings of rehearsals at Hammersmith and a from-thc-audience recording of the concert itself reveal rusty but committed performances. Not surprisingly, neither Genesis nor Peter Gabriel have released any recordings, or publicly confirmed the existence of a professional audio or visual record of the show in their archives.

Hello, I Must Be Going!

Personnel:
Phil Collins: vocals, drums, keyboards, bass pedals, percussion
Daryl Stuermer: guitars
John Giblin: bass guitar on 'I Cannot Believe It's True', 'Like China', 'You Can't Hurry Love' and 'Don't Let Him Steal Your Heart Away'
Mo Foster: bass guitar on 'It Don't Matter To Me', 'Thru These Walls'
J. Peter Robinson: piano, vibraphone and glockenspiel on 'You Can't Hurry Love'
The Phenix Horns: horns on 'I Cannot Believe It's True', 'It Don't Matter To Me' and 'The West Side': Michael Harris: trumpet; Rahmlee Michael Davis: trumpet; Don Myrick: alto and tenor saxophones; Louis 'Louie Louie' Satterfield: trombone
The Phenix Choir: additional vocals on 'I Cannot Believe It's True'
Recorded May–September 1982 at The Old Croft, Shalford, Surrey; Fisher Lane Farm, Chiddingfold, Surrey; The Townhouse, London; CBS Studios, London.
Produced by Phil Collins and Hugh Padgham.
Album release: 5 November 1982.
Highest chart placings: UK; 2; US: 8.
Side one: 'I Don't Care Anymore', 'I Cannot Believe It's True', 'Like China', 'Do You Know, Do You Care?', 'You Can't Hurry Love'
Side two: 'It Don't Matter To Me', 'Thru These Walls', 'Don't Let Him Steal Your Heart Away', 'The West Side', 'Why Can't It Wait 'Til Morning'

'Thru These Walls' b/w 'Do You Know, Do You Care?'

UK single release: October 1982. Highest chart position: 56.

'You Can't Hurry Love' b/w 'Do You Know, Do You Care?'

US single release: November 1982. Highest chart position: 10.

'You Can't Hurry Love' b/w 'I Cannot Believe It's True'
UK single release: November 1982. Highest chart position: 1.

'I Don't Care Anymore' b/w 'The West Side'
US single release: February 1983. Highest chart position: 39.

'Don't Let Him Steal Your Heart Away' b/w 'Thunder And Lightning', '...And So To F...' (live version)
UK single release: March 1983. Highest chart position: 45.

'I Cannot Believe It's True' b/w 'I Cannot Believe It's True' (live version)
US single release: April 1983. Highest chart position: 79.

'Why Can't It Wait 'Til Morning' b/w 'Like China'
UK single release: May 1983. Highest chart position: 89.

Phil Collins' second solo album takes its title from a Groucho Marx song included in the 1930 film *Animal Crackers*. 'Fundamentally, *Hello, I Must Be Going!* doesn't tick many boxes for me,' he recalled later. 'There are no real stand-out memories of writing it or even recording it. The last thing I want to do is make a second 'divorce album', but being someone who writes from the heart and not the head, right now I have no option.'

The album kicks off, almost literally, with the bombastic 'I Don't Care Any More', which more than any other song defines Collins' mid-eighties contemporary rock sound. It's an angry song directed at his ex-wife and culminates in Collins repeating the words 'no more' seventeen times. 'Cos I remember all the times I tried so hard,' he sings. 'And you laughed in my face 'cos you held all the cards. I don't care anymore.'

> If my first album [*Face Value*] was 'I'm divorced and I'm miserable,' my next one was 'I'm going to kick this fucker to bits.' By this point, I was getting letters from lawyers asking for unbelievable things. I never sat down and wrote, 'You're a bitch.' I went to school with my wife. I have a huge amount of affection for her.
> Phil Collins, *Rolling Stone*, February 2016

'I Don't Care Anymore' gave Collins his first Grammy nomination and provided an effective opening number on Collins' first two solo tours.

Speaking to the *Daily Mail* in 2015, ex-wife Andy said, 'When I asked him to stop talking and writing songs about our relationship, he said he had 'the artistic licence to write about whatever he wanted.' Basically, he was making too much money out of his divorce to worry about my feelings or his children's feelings.'

The bright, soul-influenced 'I Cannot Believe It's True' covers the same ground.

> [*Face Value's*] please-don't-go-get-out-of-my-life lyrics were so autobiographical that Collins' ex-wife might have asked for royalties. Which, in effect, she did. After *Face Value* was released, she demanded 'lots and lots of money'; he replied with a song on his next album, 'I Cannot Believe It's True'.
> *Rolling Stone*, 23 May 1985

The rocky, upbeat 'Like China' marks the return of the cockney vocal delivery last heard in 'Who Dunnit?'. The simple instrumentation and wobbly guitar solo provide a welcome contrast to the parping horns of 'It Don't Matter To Me', even if the song tends to drag on for a minute or two more than necessary. 'Do You Know, Do You Care?' sounds like a dry run for Genesis' 'Mama'. Collins' fondness for instrumentals is sated with the jazzy 'The West Side', which complements 'Hand In Hand' from *Face Value*.

The album's first single, 'Thru These Walls' is an obvious rewrite of 'In The Air Tonight' with several repeats of that famous drum fill but with none of the tension of his biggest solo hit thus far. It reached a lowly 56 in the UK and was not even released as a single in America.

'On my part', Collins writes, 'there's no panic but a little disappointment, and some resignation. Luckily, Motown saves me, as it had done so often in my youth — as a teenager, the label and its artists were the soundtrack of my life. Paying tribute, I include on *Hello, I Must Be Going!* a cover of 'You Can't Hurry Love.' I think of it as one of the forgotten Supremes songs, a bit of a dark horse; the likes of 'You Keep Me Hangin' On' and 'Stop in the Name of Love' seemed to get the most plays and the most affection. 'You Can't Hurry Love' finger-snaps to number one in the UK. It's the only hit from the album (it also reaches number 10 in the US and pushes *Hello, I Must Be Going!* to number one in Britain).'

'That song, in its own unappealing way,' writes Steven Hyden in *The Ringer* (2016), 'encapsulates the '80s — the erasure of African Americans by white mainstream rockers, the bloodless sanitization of the '60s, the boomer self-obsession, the extremely bad taste.'

Three further singles were less successful. The gentle piano ballad 'Don't Let Him Steal Your Heart Away', released in the UK in March 1983, crawled to number 45. If this had been a follow-up to, say, 'Against All Odds (Take A Look At Me Now)', it would surely be regarded as classic Collins. 'I Cannot Believe It's True' would barely trouble US chart compilers, reaching only as high as number 79. Finally, the maudlin 'Why Can't It Wait 'Til Morning' crawled to a lowly number 89 after UK release in May 1983. By this time, the next Genesis album had been recorded.

Hammersmith With John Martyn

In mid-October 1982, Collins travelled to Sweden for promotion work with Frida. He returned to play drums on a few songs at a John Martyn gig at the Hammersmith Odeon on 22 October. They also sang 'Sweet Little Mystery' together.

'Phil was sorting the sound out, running around in the soundcheck,' said Martyn's drummer Jeff Allen. 'It was already a good gig, but it went through the roof when he came on and sang.'

Phil Collins In Concert With The Fabulous Jacuzzis And The One Neat Guy

Hello, I Must Be Going! was released on 5 November 1982. A short European tour in the last two weeks of the month concluded with four nights at the Hammersmith Odeon. A further twelve dates before the end of the year in smallish venues in Canada and the US saw Collins perform seventeen of the twenty-two songs from his first two solo albums: 'I Don't Care Anymore', 'Thunder And Lightning', 'I Cannot Believe It's True', 'This Must Be Love', 'Thru These Walls', 'I Missed Again', 'Behind The Lines', 'You Know What I Mean', 'The Roof Is Leaking', 'Don't Let Him Steal Your Heart Away', 'The West Side', 'If Leaving Me Is Easy', 'In The Air Tonight', 'Like China', 'You Can't Hurry Love', 'It Don't Matter To Me' and 'Hand In Hand', with a two-song encore of the Brand X song '...And So To F...' and a cover of 'People Get Ready' by The Impressions. Occasional calls for 'Supper's Ready' would prompt Collins to chirp a highly-abridged ten-second version.

Phil's band include long-time Genesis touring members Daryl Stuermer and Chester Thompson on guitar and drums, with Mo Foster (bass), Peter Robinson (keyboards) and the Phenix Horns. With the exception of

Thompson, these were the musicians Collins had hired for *Something's Going On* earlier in the year.

There is a handful of live recordings available from the tour. 'If Leaving Me Is Easy' was recorded at the Berkeley Community Theatre in San Francisco on 16 December 1982. This is included on the 2016 reissue of *Face Value* (credited as a 1985 performance) along with a recording of '... And So To F...' from either the same concert or, more likely, from Perkin's Palace in Pasadena a few days later. The Pasadena concert was released on VHS in 1983 and provided live versions of 'Don't Let Him Steal Your Heart Away' (on the UK 12" vinyl single only) and 'I Cannot Believe It's True' (released as the b-side of the studio version). The latter recording is more easily heard on the 2016 reissue of *Hello, I Must Be Going!*, together with versions of 'People Get Ready' and 'Thru These Walls' from Pasadena.

1983

The Principle of Moments and Scenario

It's difficult to imagine anyone else sitting in with artists as diverse as Robert Plant and Al Di Meola – and what's more, fitting them around a very busy schedule as a solo artist and member of one of the world's top-selling rock groups. The second leg of the *Hello, I Must Be Going!* Tour took in thirty dates across North America between 22 January and 20 February 1983, and Genesis reconvened in March for writing and recording. These sessions, therefore, most likely date from the first three weeks of 1983 and/or in early spring 1983.

Robert Plant's second solo album, *The Principle of Moments,* would be recorded back at Rockfield. Again, Collins plays on three-quarters of the tracks. *The Principle of Moments* was released on 11 July 1983, reaching number seven in the UK and number eight in the US. The opening track, the hard-rocking 'Other Arms', was a popular track on AOR radio in the US, reaching number one on the Billboard Mainstream Rock chart. It's close to Plant's Led Zeppelin back catalogue, with Collins' hammering drums and Robbie Blunt's spiky guitar licks leavened by some vocal harmonies. 'In The Mood' is slower and moodier. It was a reasonable hit single in the US and Collins' drumming is sharp, pushing the beat. The syncopated mid-paced 'Messin' With The Mekon' has some characteristic Collins drum fills and the massive 'Thru' With The Two Step' uses Collins' heavily reverbed signature sound. 'Horizontal Departure' – which gathers pace like a runaway truck – has stellar performances from Plant, Blunt and Collins. The closing song, the stately 'Big Log,' is, by some measure, Plant's biggest hit as either a solo artist or group member – number eleven in the UK and twenty in the US. Collins is credited as the drummer, although it sounds like a drum machine throughout. The unreleased 'Turnaround' was also recorded during these sessions.

Jazz guitarist Di Meola brought together musicians of rare skill for his *Scenario* album. The likes of Jan Hammer, Tony Levin, Bill Bruford and Phil Collins are employed across various tracks, although Collins plays only on 'Island Dreamer'. The album was recorded at Caribou Ranch in Nederland, Colorado. Exact dates for the sessions have not been confirmed, but it seems unlikely that Collins would have travelled to the central US to play on a single song, so it's probable that 'Island Dreamer' was recorded during a free date on Collins' solo tours between December 1982 and February 1983. 'Island Dreamer' has a bubbling drum machine, snappy snare and a light reggae feel, which moves uncomfortably close to lift muzak.

Genesis

Personnel:
Tony Banks: keyboards, backing vocals
Mike Rutherford: guitars, bass guitars, backing vocals
Phil Collins: drums, percussion, lead vocals
Recorded March–May 1983 at The Farm, Chiddingfold, Surrey.
Produced by Genesis and Hugh Padgham.
Album release: 3 October 1983.
Highest chart placings: UK: 1; US: 9.
Side one: 'Mama', 'That's All', 'Home By The Sea', 'Second Home By The Sea'
Side two: 'Illegal Alien', 'Taking It All Too Hard', 'Just A Job To Do', 'Silver Rainbow', 'It's Gonna Get Better'

'Mama' b/w 'It's Gonna Get Better'

Single release: August 1983. Highest chart positions: UK: 4; US: 73.
12" single includes extended versions of both songs.

'That's All' b/w 'Taking It All Too Hard'

UK single release: October 1983. Highest chart position: 16.
12" single adds a live version of 'Firth Of Fifth' from 29 November 1981.

'That's All' b/w 'Second Home By The Sea'

US single release: October 1983. Highest chart position: 6.

'Illegal Alien' b/w 'Turn It On Again (live)'

Single release: January 1984. Highest chart positions: UK: 46; US: 44.
The 12" single includes 'Turn It On Again' recorded in Philadelphia on 27 November 1983. This includes the medley of 'Everybody Needs Somebody to Love', '(I Can't Get No) Satisfaction', 'The Last Time', 'All Day and All of the Night' and 'In the Midnight Hour'. The 7" single edits out this medley.

'Taking It All Too Hard' b/w 'Silver Rainbow'

US single release: June 1984. Highest chart position: 50.

The three members of Genesis reconvened at the Farm in March 1983, seven months after the conclusion of the Three Sides Encore tour. Rutherford's *Acting Very Strange* had been released the previous September and Banks' *The Fugitive* would follow mid-way through sessions for Genesis' twelfth album. Starting with no pre-written music, the band started several weeks of sessions with three days of jamming.

Phil said in *Genesis: Peter Gabriel, Phil Collins & Beyond*, in 1984:

> We moved into [the studio] with no music written at all. We just had the idea that we would start mucking about – jamming, or whatever you want to call it – and record at the same time. We just put some drum machine patterns on ... I started singing, Mike started playing, Tony started playing... and things like 'Mama' came out.

Ideas coalesced and songs began to form. 'We didn't actually just settle for the first thing we recorded,' Collins wrote later. 'If something was wrong, we'd say 'Let's go back and do it again'. We found a way that the three of us really wanted to work.'And that approach would bear fruit. *Genesis* contains both the band's biggest ever UK hit single ('Mama') and their biggest US hit thus far ('That's All').

The dark, brooding, sinister and very original 'Mama' opens the album with a cinematic sweep. It reached number four in the UK on 17 September 1983 behind a top three consisting of 'Red Red Wine' by UB40, 'Tonight I Celebrate My Love For You' by Peabo Bryson and Roberta Flack, and 'Karma Chameleon' by Culture Club – proof, if needed, of the variety in the UK singles chart at the time.

'Mama' starts with Rutherford's distorted, distinctive drum machine pattern, marking the offbeat and providing the idiosyncratic opening sounds to an album that matches experimentation with commercialism. The introduction of the synthesiser chords at 3.17 and the trademark gated drum sounds from 4.10 recall 'In The Air Tonight', and, likewise, lift the song measurably. Collins' vocal performance is excellent, with hints of John Lennon in the heavy echo and the pleading 'mama, don't go'.

> 'Mama' offers brainy prog, and pure pop, and big beats, and discomfiting terror, and comforting '80s cheese. It's all of those things, and never just one of those things.
>
> Steven Hyden, *The Ringer*, 2018

The live version is even better – especially as the powerful opening number for the massive 1986-1987 *Invisible Touch* tour. For collectors, the single edit removes forty seconds by editing the final verse, the radio edit chops out another minute and the 12" mix extends the song by forty seconds with a longer fade-out.

An alternative 'work in progress' version, which lasts almost eleven minutes, is included in the *Archive #2* box set. The lyrics are sketchy, but the arrangement is hypnotic.

The wonderful 'That's All' has a loping piano riff reminiscent of The Beatles' 'Martha My Dear'. Even the drums are 100% Ringo. The radio-friendly rhythm matches an effortless commerciality. 'That's All' was Genesis' first US top tenner, reaching number six. The video was directed by Jim Yukich, the beginning of a long and fruitful career as director of many promos and documentaries for both Genesis and Phil Collins until 2003.

'Home By The Sea' and 'Second Home By The Sea' are the perfect bridge between the 'old' and 'new' Genesis, retaining the structure of the band's epics of the 1970s but utilising a very modern production sound.

Phil Collins:

> What we did on a song like 'Home By The Sea' was to record with a programmed drum machine. Tony would play a guide keyboard part, Mike would play a guide guitar part, and I'd sing a guide vocal. If we liked what we got, we would then go in and record.

As the opening 'Home By The Sea' fades, we have a linking section which moves to an instrumental passage based on Collin's driving drum pattern edited from an hour of improvisation.

> An eerie and atmospheric midsection provides the bridge to one of the band's best instrumentals driven by a soaring melodic synth solo from Banks and propelled along by Collins' thunderous Simmons drum lick.
> Steve Aldous, *The Songs of Genesis: A Complete Guide to the Studio Recordings* (2020)

After a short, tight guitar solo, the piece ends with a reprise of the main theme and verse of 'Home By The Sea'. Despite not being an instrumental, 'Second Home By The Sea' was nominated as Best Rock

Above: Phil Collins singing on stage with Genesis in 1981.

Right: A moody Phil in a 1989 publicity shot.

Left: For better or worse, *Duke* marks the end of the dominating 'progressive' period in Genesis' music. (*Charisma / Universal Music Group*)

Right: Peter Gabriel's third self-titled solo album introduced the world to 'that' drum sound. (*Charisma / Universal Music Group*)

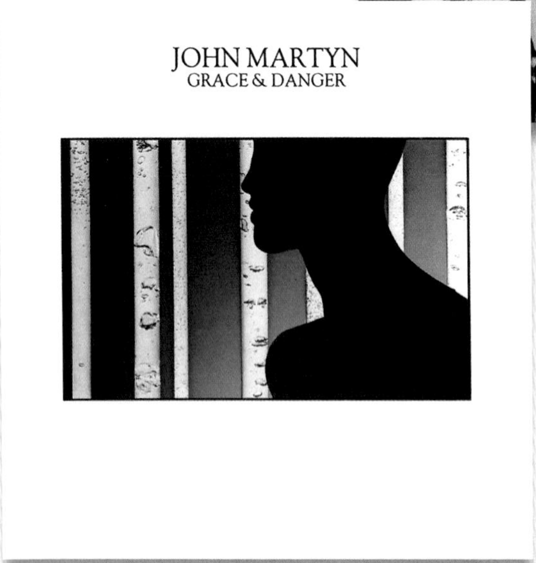

Left: The elegant *Grace and Danger* by John Martyn. 'I fell in love with John and his music during these sessions,' said Collins later. (*Island / Universal Music Group*)

This page: Three huge albums released in 1981-1982: *Face Value*, *Abacab* and *Hello, I Must Be Going!*. *Abacab* lost Genesis lots of fans but gained many more. (*Charisma / Virgin / Universal Music Group*)

This page: Water damage from a rainy day is evident on the programme from the Six Of The Best concert which reunited Genesis with Peter Gabriel. (*Stuart Nicholson collection*)

Right: Beginning with no pre-written music, Genesis started several weeks of sessions with three days of jamming. The resultant album was focussed and very commercial. (*Charisma / Virgin / Universal Music Group*)

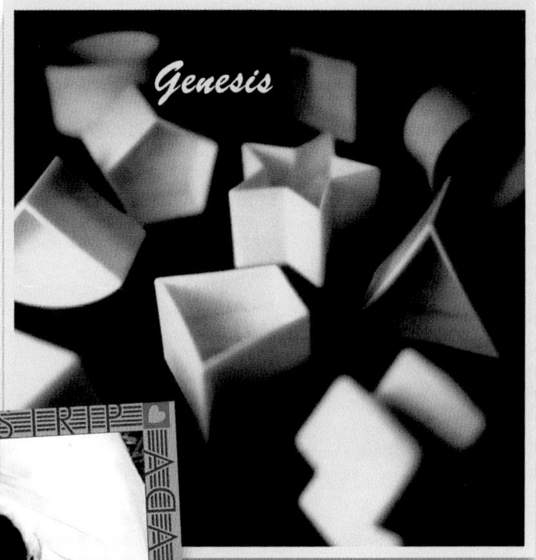

Left and below: Collins continued varied session work in 1983: working with artists as diverse as Adam Ant and Robert Plant. (*Columbia / Sony Music Entertainment, Atlantic Records Group*)

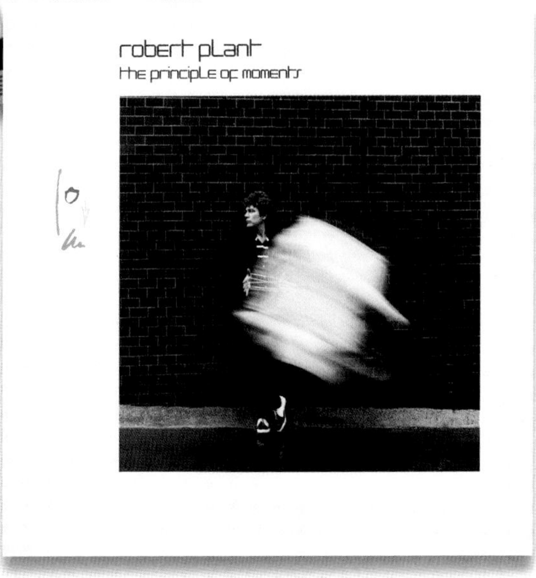

Left: 'In The Air Tonight', the surprise hit that changed everything. (*Virgin / Universal Music Group*)

Right: Phil sings 'Misunderstanding', Genesis' biggest hit to date in the US, and a number one in Canada. (*Charisma / Universal Music Group*)

Left: The video for 'Abacab', Genesis' third top tenner in the UK. (*Charisma / Universal Music Group*)

Right: 'Mama'. Genesis' most successful single in the UK. (*Charisma / Virgin / Universal Music Group*)

Left: At Live Aid. 'Good afternoon Wembley, good afternoon Philadelphia, good afternoon the world.' (*Rhino*)

Right: 'I was in England this afternoon. Funny old world, innit?' (*Rhino*)

Left: 'Against All Odds' was Collin's solo breakthrough in the US. It was the first of his seven solo number one hits between spring 1984 and late 1989. (*Virgin / Universal Music Group*)

Right: Collins was the drummer on 'Do They Know It's Christmas', the charity single that kickstarted Live Aid. It remained the UK's biggest-selling single for fifteen years. (*Phonogram / PolyGram*)

Left: *No Jacket Required*; an album that seems hermetically sealed in the mid-eighties. (*Virgin / Universal Music Group*)

Right: 'Separate Lives' was released in November 1985, reaching number four in the UK and securing Collins' third chart-topper of the year in the US. (*Virgin / Universal Music Group*)

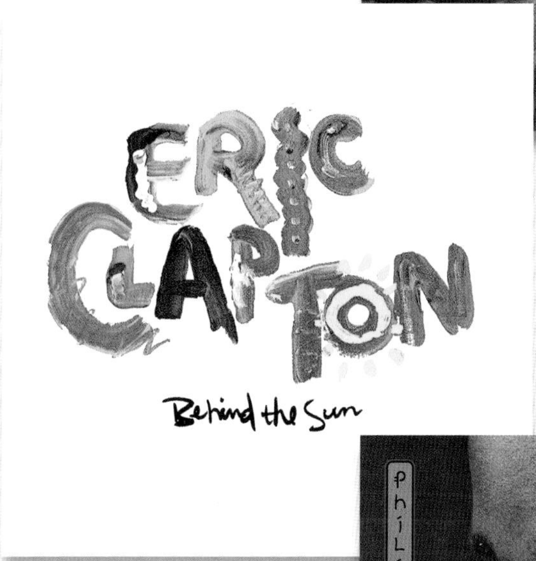

Left and below: Collins worked successfully with Eric Clapton and Philip Bailey, producing major hit albums for them in 1985. (*Duck / Warner Music Group, Columbia / Sony Music Entertainment*)

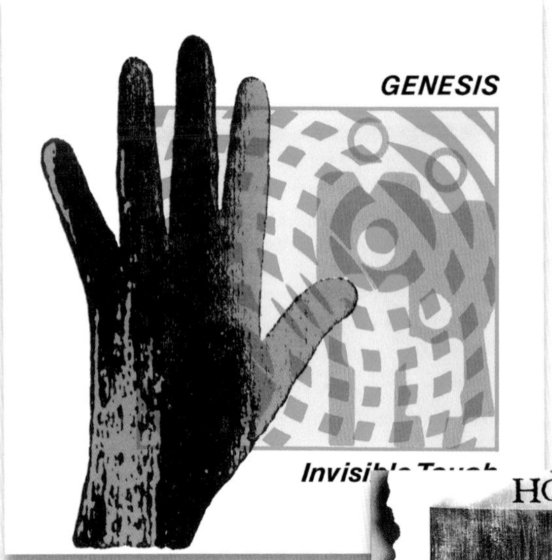

Left: *Invisible Touch* sold over six million copies in the US, the fourth best-selling album there by a British group in the 1980s. (*Virgin / Universal Music Group*)

Right and below: Howard Jones and Chaka Khan benefitted from Collins' production and/ or drumming skills in 1985-1986. (*WEA / Warner Bros / Warner Music Group*

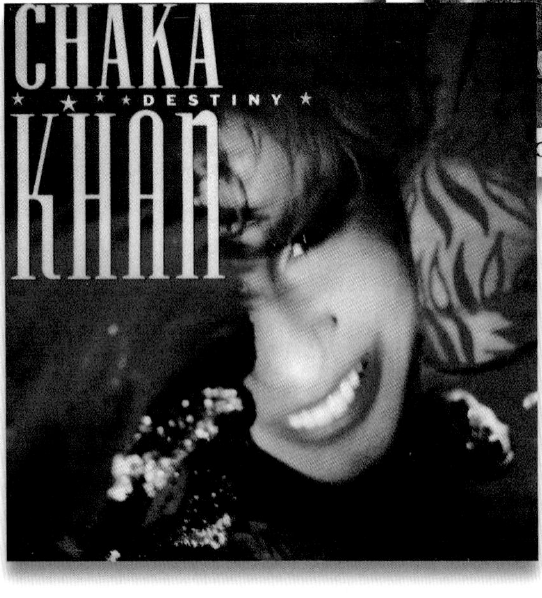

This page: Collins fitted time around 1986 tour commitments to record with Paul McCartney, Eric Clapton and Tina Turner. (*Parlophone / Duck / Capitol / Warner Music Group*)

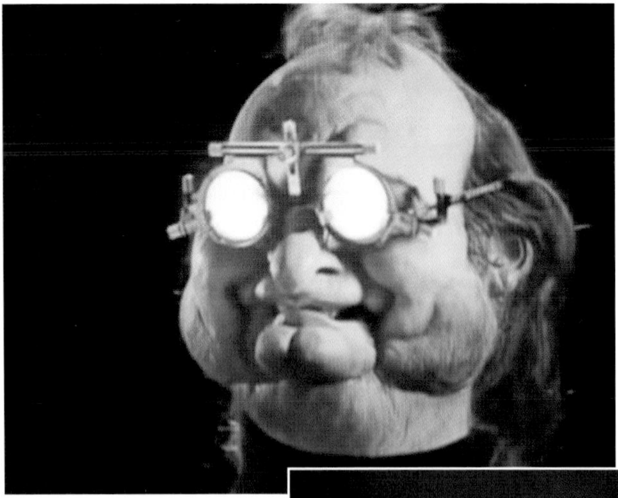

Left: Phil's puppet from the 'Land of Confusion' video which was nominated for MTV Video of the Year in 1987. (*Virgin / Universal Music Group*)

Right: 'Invisible Touch', Genesis' only number one single in America. (*Virgin / Universal Music Group*)

Left: Philip Bailey and Phil Collins sing 'Easy Lover' in 1984. (*BBC*)

This page: Phil appears on *Top Of The Pops* in 1981, 1985 and 1989 performing 'In The Air Tonight', 'Take Me Home' and 'Another Day In Paradise'. (*BBC*)

Left: 'Land Of Confusion'; a huge hit for Genesis as 1986 turned into 1987. (*Virgin / Universal Music Group*)

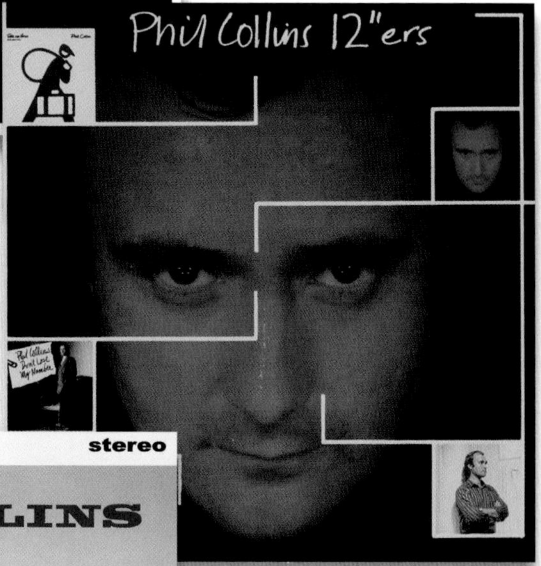

Right: With Collins away with Genesis on tour for the first half of 1987, Virgin released a stop-gap compilation of 12" singles. (*Virgin / Universal Music Group*)

Left: Phil Collins spent the first few months of 1988 filming *Buster*. The soundtrack album and associated single 'A Groovy Kind of Love' were big sellers around the world. (*Virgin / Universal Music Group*)

This page: Sessions from 1989: Stephen Bishop, Tears for Fears and Eric Clapton. (*Atlantic, Fontana / Universal Music Group, Duck / Warner Music Group*)

Left: *But Seriously...* 'You can divine my state of mind by my expression on the cover art,' Collins wrote. 'I'm wearing my heart, and my seriousness, on my album sleeve.' (*Virgin / Universal Music Group*)

Right and below: Phil and pal Eric Clapton in the toe-curling promotional video for 'I Wish It Would Rain Down'. (*Virgin / Universal Music Group*)

Instrumental Performance at the 1984 Grammies. The award was given to Ray Parker Jr for 'Ghostbusters', the non-vocal b-side of his hit single.

'Home By The Sea' and 'Second Home By The Sea' conclude 23 minutes of the first side of the original vinyl release and represents post-*Abacab* Genesis at their very best. 'Mama' and 'Home By The Sea / Second Home By The Sea' would feature in every future Genesis set-list, even those without Phil Collins.

Side two of the original album moves the listener from the sublime to the ridiculous for the tongue-in-cheek and much-derided 'Illegal Alien'. It's a Mike Rutherford song, so we cannot blame Phil Collins for the embarrassing lyrics, which are meant to be light-hearted and humorous, but come across as borderline racist. However, we cannot forgive Collins' cod-Mexican accent. The song includes lines such as 'I've got a sister who'd be willing to oblige / She will do anything now to help me get to the outside'.

Thankfully, the beautiful acoustic ballad 'Taking It All Too Hard', a minor US single in June 1984, sounds a lot like Collins' solo work and points towards 'In Too Deep' on *Invisible Touch* as well as later songs such as 'Never A Time' and 'Hold On My Heart'. Collins' lyrics are direct, with a wry play on 'to heart'/'too hard'.

> No, not this confused again
> No, not the same mistakes again
> You're taking it all to heart
> You're taking it all too hard

The album continues with two lesser-known songs: 'Just A Job To Do' and 'Silver Rainbow'. 'Just A Job To Do' deserves to be better known: catchy and up-tempo, almost funky with a very commercial chorus. It's perhaps too close to 'Don't Lose My Number' from *Hello, I Must Be Going!*, but still sounds like a potential hit. Banks' 'Silver Rainbow', a song about sex, employs a pulsating Adam Ant drum pattern: 'Adam And' was the song's working title and Collins would work with Ant a few months after the *Genesis* sessions. 'Just A Job To Do' and 'Silver Rainbow' are the only songs from *Genesis* never to have been performed in concert by the band.

Genesis closes on a high note with the wonderful, atmospheric, optimistic 'It's Gonna Get Better', which reworks the feel of 'Watcher Of The Skies' but sounds thoroughly modern. When released as the b-side to 'Mama', 'It's Gonna Get Better' was extended to 6.36 for the 12" single with an extra chorus. The live version used this same arrangement which suggests that this was the original arrangement before it was edited down for album release.

As with *Abacab*, *Genesis* is two or three songs short of being a classic. It garnered one of the band's handful of Grammy nominations for Album of the Year. Lionel Richie took the gong for *Can't Slow Down*.

Brett Elliot Easton's horrifying central character in the novel *American Psycho* (1991) waxes lyrical about *Genesis* in a psychotic screed which is full of intentional faux pas.

> Hugh Padgham produced next an even less conceptual effort, simply called *Genesis* (Atlantic; 1983), and though it's a fine album, a lot of it now seems too derivative for my tastes. 'That's All' sounds like 'Misunderstanding,' 'Taking It All Too Hard' reminds me of 'Throwing It All Away.' It also seems less jazzy than its predecessors and more of an eighties pop album, more rock 'n' roll. Padgham does a brilliant job of producing, but the material is weaker than usual and you can sense the strain. It opens with the autobiographical 'Mama,' that's both strange and touching, though I couldn't tell if the singer was talking about his actual mother or to a girl he likes to call 'Mama.' 'That's All' is a lover's lament about being ignored and beaten down by an unreceptive partner; despite the despairing tone, it's got a bright sing-along melody that makes the song less depressing than it probably needed to be. 'That's All' is the best tune on the album, but Phil's voice is strongest on 'House by the Sea,' whose lyrics are, however, too stream-of-consciousness to make much sense. It might be about growing up and accepting adulthood, but it's unclear; at any rate, its second instrumental part puts the song more in focus for me and Mike Banks gets to show off his virtuosic guitar skills while Tom Rutherford washes the tracks over with dreamy synthesizers, and when Phil repeats the song's third verse at the end it can give you chills. Even if the lyrics seem a tiny bit generic to some, Phil's voice is so confident (heavily influenced by Peter Gabriel, who never made an album this polished and heartfelt himself) that he makes us believe in glorious possibilities.

Sessions With Adam Ant, And On Tour With Percy

With a short gap in his schedule between the completion of *Genesis* and rehearsals for the next Genesis tour, Collins recorded with Adam Ant in Stockholm and went on the road with Robert Plant.

Fast fading 'dandy highwayman' Adam Ant had had his biggest successes in 1980-1981, scoring nine top ten hits (and two numbers ones) with the likes of 'Dog Eat Dog', 'Ant Music', 'Kings Of The Wild Frontier', 'Stand And Deliver', 'Prince Charming' and 'Ant Rap'. He continued this run with the solo number one 'Goody Two Shoes' in mid-1982. Ant released his second solo album *Strip* in November 1983, recorded at Polar Music in Stockholm earlier that year. Collins played on and co-produced two tracks: 'Puss 'n Boots' and 'Strip'; both songs were released as singles. 'Puss 'n' Boots' (October 1983) reached a respectable number five on the UK chart, becoming Ant's final top 10 hit. Frida from Abba performs the female spoken word part on 'Strip'. The very cheesy video was banned by the B.B.C. due to Ant's saucy semi-naked revelling with former Miss World Mary Stavin.

Rehearsals for the Robert Plant tour were held at the Dallas Communications Complex Studios in Irving in mid-August. The tour started on 26 August in Peoria, Illinois and ended six weeks later in Vancouver, British Columbia. Plant elected only to play tracks from his solo albums, ignoring Led Zeppelin's oeuvre entirely.

'That was a great experience,' Collins told Kamin and Goddard in 1984. 'It's great fun to play another kind of music, to be honest. You know it brings out a side of me … that I haven't been able to.'

At least one show was filmed: Montreal, 8 September 1983. An amateur recording, available on YouTube at the time of writing, proves that Phil Collins was a perfect fit for Plant's new music.

Live versions of 'Pledge Pin' and 'Horizontal Departure' from The Summit, Houston on 20 September 1983 were later released on the UK 12" single 'In The Mood'. Four further tracks from this concert were made available on the 2007 re-issues of *Pictures At Eleven* and *Principles Of Moments*: 'Like I've Never Been Gone', 'In The Mood', 'Thru' With The Two Step', and a cover of Bob Marley's 'Lively Up Yourself'.

The Mama Tour

Genesis' Mama tour crossed the US for six weeks in November and December 1983, playing mostly large indoor venues. The set was fairly static, offering plenty to appease older fans and most of the new album: 'Dodo/Lurker', 'Abacab', 'That's All', 'Mama', a medley of 'Eleventh Earl of Mar', 'Squonk' and 'Firth Of Fifth', then 'Illegal Alien', 'Man On The Corner', 'Who Dunnit?', 'Home By The Sea / Second Home By The Sea', 'The Carpet Crawlers', 'Keep It Dark', 'It's Gonna Get Better', 'Follow You

Follow Me', a medley of 'In The Cage' with parts of 'The Cinema Show', '...In That Quiet Earth', 'The Colony Of Slippermen' and 'Afterglow', then the 'Drum Duet' and 'Los Endos' to close out the main set. Encores comprised 'Misunderstanding' and 'Turn It On Again'. This was the last tour to include 'Eleventh Earl Of Mar', a regular since 1976. Despite, or perversely perhaps because of, its unpopularity, the annoying 'Who Dunnit?' remained in the setlist.

Only one performance from this leg of the tour has been officially released. 'Turn It On Again' from the Philadelphia Spectrum on 27 November 1983 was used as the b-side to the 'Illegal Alien' single in late January 1984. This includes the pop medley interlude of 'Everybody Needs Somebody To Love', '(I Can't Get No) Satisfaction', 'The Last Time', 'All Day And All Of The Night' and 'In The Midnight Hour'. To frustrate collectors, the 7" and 12" versions use different edits. Seven songs recorded during rehearsals are included on the *1983-1998* box set.

1984

Mama Tour – Second Leg

The second leg of the Mama tour took in another thirty dates across the US and Canada in January and February 1984. Five dates back in the UK in Birmingham closed out the tour. These were the only concerts outside North America. The setlists were very similar to the first leg, although the 'old medley' now included elements from 'The Lamb Lies Down On Broadway' and 'The Musical Box'.

Two live recordings from this tour can be heard on the *Archive #2* box set, both from the Forum, Los Angeles, on 14 January 1984: 'Illegal Alien' and 'It's Gonna Get Better'. It's likely that the live recordings of 'Home By The Sea / Second Home By The Sea' and 'That's All' released in 1992 on the 'Hold On My Heart' and 'I Can't Dance' CD singles date from this series of concerts.

Genesis' concerts at the Birmingham N.E.C. Arena in February 1984 were recorded and filmed: around two-thirds of the set was released as a home video *Genesis Live: The Mama Tour* in October 1985 and later on DVD. This was the last Genesis activity until summer 1985, by which time Phil Collins was a household name.

'Against All Odds (Take A Look At Me Now)'

'Against All Odds (Take A Look At Me Now)', released in March 1984, was Collin's solo breakthrough in the US. It was the first of his seven US solo number one hits between spring 1984 and late 1989. Collins met film director Taylor Hackford after a Genesis concert in Chicago at the end of 1982. Hackford was hot after the success off An Officer and a Gentleman and was working on a new project, Against All Odds. Collins offered him an unfinished song with the title 'How Can You Just Sit There?'

The orchestral backing track, with piano performed by session musician Rob Mounsey, was recorded at RCA Studios in New York in spring 1983 under the supervision of producer and arranger Arif Mardin. Collins added his drums and vocals in Los Angeles and the video was shot as Collins continued his trek with Genesis across the US.

Collins wrote in his memoirs:

> The director is thrilled with the end result, and I'm pretty pleased, too. In a short space of time I seem to have become known as a writer who can crystallize emotional turmoil. I'm the Phil Collins of Genesis lore, but

> to more and more people, I'm the Phil Collins who's written 'In The Air Tonight' and 'Don't Let Him Steal Your Heart Away,' who can write with space, and also with dramatic, cinematic sweep. The song is big, way bigger than the film. It's now viewed as a paradigm of the eighties power ballad, that phenomenon from the decade when the hair was big, the emotions were bigger, but the shoulder pads were biggest of all.

As Collins told *Rolling Stone* in 2016: 'It was basically like saying, 'Here's $10 million. Would you want it?' I had already written the lyrics, before I saw the film.'

The song has since been covered as a duet by Mariah Carey and Westlife (2000) and by X-Factor winner Steve Brookstein (2005). Both were UK number one hits.

For Genesis completists, the soundtrack album released in early 1984 includes the Peter Gabriel track 'Walk Through The Fire' and Mike Rutherford's solo song 'Making A Big Mistake', both exclusive to this album.

Collins: 'I'd ignored 'Against All Odds (Take A Look At Me Now)' when I was recording *Face Value*, viewing it as a B-side at best. Then it becomes my first American number one, wins my first Grammy and secures my first Oscar nomination.'

Collins' original wordless demo was released on the 2016 deluxe reissue of *Face Value*.

Behind The Sun and Banded Together

Phil Collins and Eric Clapton had become friendly over the previous few years. They had first met when Collins was working with John Martyn in 1979, as Collins writes in his autobiography:

> One tiring day during the *Grace & Danger* sessions, [John Martyn] is looking for something to, ah, brighten up his day and thinks Eric can help. So John calls and asks if the pair of us can come over to Eric's house in Ewhurst. Eric must have said no—John is the kind of chap who has a tendency to overstay his welcome, and here he's suggesting popping down to score with me, a complete stranger. So we meet in a pub in Guildford. Eric doesn't know me from a bar of soap, but I do remember sitting with a pint of Guinness opposite one of my heroes. Me, quaffing pints in the pub, with the guy I'd idolized at the Marquee…

By the end of the year, Clapton and Collins are close friends. Clapton sees Collins perform for the first time in at London's Hammersmith Odeon on 28 March 1980.

Four years later…

'I was back on the treadmill looking for another formula for a successful album,' Clapton recalled in his own candid memoirs. '[Manager] Roger [Forrester's] suggestion was a collaboration with Phil Collins, who was riding high at the time. Though I wasn't a fan of Genesis, Phil and I had become good friends over the years; a friendship strengthened during the break-up of his marriage to his first wife, Andrea, when he used to come over to Hurtwood and pour his heart out to Pattie and me. Though at first Roger's plan just seemed like a pretty obvious marketing ploy, in the end, I decided it wasn't such a bad idea.'

Phil Collins said in *Playboy* in 1986:

> If someone like Clapton asks me to produce him, I'm completely flattered. It's like I couldn't say number I learn a lot, too. With Clapton, well, Eric has been one of my best friends for some time, and one day he just called me up. I was blown away by it. 'My God, Eric Clapton wants me to produce him.' Even though we're best mates, he's still Eric Clapton. I used to play Cream songs in my school band. Anyway, the fashion of music keeps changing, and people like Eric sort of get left behind a bit in people's minds, if nothing else. I saw producing his records as an opportunity to make people realize that this guy is still a fantastic guitar player and he's got a great voice.

'Eric's last couple of albums were a little bland, production-wise,' Collins said in 1985. 'So when he asked me to produce him, I thought it would be a great chance to shake up his music and make it stand again. He had written some great songs, was off the booze, playing and singing better than ever.'

The album was recorded in spring 1984 at George Martin's Air Studios in Montserrat. 'Eric and I got really close.' Collins told Ray Coleman. 'It was a very enjoyable time.'

The pounding production marks out the territory for *Behind The Sun* – an 80s sound full of parping synthesisers, chorus-laden guitar sounds, Collins' rolling drums and plenty of reverb.

Thirteen songs were recorded, including the Australia-only single, 'You Don't Know Like I Know', released in November 1984, jointly credited to

Clapton and Collins. This is a superb cover of the classic Sam and Dave song from 1966, which has only ever been released on 7" single. Clapton and Collins sing well together, and it's a shame that this hasn't been more widely distributed.

Clapton and Collins co-wrote the fragile 'Never Make You Cry'. 'I was surprised to be asked [to write the lyrics for the verses]', Collins told Ray Coleman. 'I thought a love song is the one kind of song you would normally want to do yourself, but Eric didn't want to or couldn't.'

The delicate title track was the last song recorded for the album, as Collins recalls:

> Eric rings me one day: 'I've written a song that has to be on the record.' He comes round to Old Croft [Collins' house] with his guitar and sings it to me. I'm floored. It's fantastic, and clearly deeply personal and pained. I say, 'How are we going to record this? The sessions are over; the album's done, everyone's gone home.' Eric says, 'We'll do it now.' He plays it once or twice, no more, and I record it. The meters are moving: that's good. Then I have to record his vocal. Again I see the meters moving: that's a relief. Now we have to mix it. It's only him and the guitar, but for mood I put a little synth on it, nothing more than sustained strings. Old Croft is definitely not a good mixing studio, but Eric likes what he hears.

And then, such was the music industry at that time, Clapton's record label Warner Brothers insisted that further recording sessions were needed, as the album was not commercial enough. 'I spoke to Eric,' Collins wrote, 'and he was fuming. We had all felt so solid about the album, and suddenly these people, who had no input at all when the record was being made, came in and said that there were no singles.'

Clapton recorded several more songs, without Collins' involvement, in Los Angeles. *Behind The Sun* was a big success. Its commercial sound and hit single 'Forever Man' pushed the album into the UK top ten – Clapton's highest singles chart placing for eleven years. The album was released in March 1985 and returned Clapton to the album chart top ten for the first time in nine years. Two of the rejected Collins-produced songs from the Monserrat sessions were released as b-sides: 'Too Bad' and 'Jailbait'.

In the same period, Collins drummed on the track 'Mandela' by American jazz guitarist Lee Ritenour who was taking an ill-advised foray into adult pop on his 1984 album *Banded Together* recorded at Starlight Studios in Tracy, sixty miles east of San Francisco. Vocals are by

John Massaro, formerly of Steve Miller Band. Phil Collins provides his trademark gated drum sound through an overlong and forgettable track.

Ritenour would later form the contemporary jazz band Fourplay with bassist Nathan East. Fourplay would record a terrific version of 'Why Can't It Wait Till Morning' (originally from *Hello, I Must Be Going!*) with Collins himself on lead vocals for their 1995 album *Elixir*.

Chinese Wall + 'Easy Lover'

Chinese Wall was the third solo album by Earth, Wind and Fire vocalist Philip Bailey. It was recorded in the summer of 1984 at the Townhouse with overdubs in Los Angeles.

'I always loved Earth, Wind and Fire,' Collins told *Rolling Stone* in 2016, 'and in 1984 I was asked if I would produce Philip Bailey's solo album. People were leaning on him racially — 'Don't come back with a white album. You're one of us.' So Philip got Nathan East to play on it also. We hit some rocky ground early on, but we worked everything out.'

Collins: 'Near the end of the sessions, Philip said, 'We haven't written anything together on this album.' So we just started having a jam one night, and went round and round and turned it into a verse and a chorus. We recorded it that night so we wouldn't forget it. That song doesn't sound like any particular era. It's just fantastic.''

Phil Collins said in *Playboy* in 1986:

> Bailey got a lot of flak for being produced by someone who is white. There was this paranoia that the album would not be played by black stations. In this business, you find out that there is more racism on the black side of the fence than on the white side. They didn't want to know about me, because I'm white. We did it, though, and broke down some of those walls. 'Easy Lover' was a black hit and a pop hit and my song 'Sussudio' was a number-three record on the black charts as a result of the thing's being opened up by 'Easy Lover'. The race thing is not great on either side. If you're Prince or Lionel Richie, you can get played on MTV, but not many other black artists can. The reason I was on the video for 'Easy Lover' was that I knew it wouldn't be shown if it was just Phil Bailey. Barriers will break down as there is more crossover, but they are slow to break down.

'Easy Lover' is a sublime mix of R & B, pop and rock, combining Collins' booming drums, Philip Bailey's extraordinary falsetto, a grinding rock-

jazz guitar solo from Daryl Stuermer and a very catchy chorus. The video cleverly plays up Collins' unhip persona next to the slick Bailey. 'Easy Lover' reached number two in the US, kept off the top by Foreigner's 'I Want to Know What Love Is', and hit number one in the UK

> One of the most memorable scenes from *The Assassination of Gianni Versace: American Crime Story,* [the] brilliant and underwatched 2018 miniseries, concerns Andrew Cunanan (Darren Criss) and a wealthy older man who thinks he has hired Cunanan to have sex with him in his Miami hotel room. What the man doesn't know is that Cunanan is a fugitive serial killer who will soon murder the world's most famous fashion designer. Cunanan has decided to torture his would-be john with some duct tape, a pair of scissors, and 'Easy Lover', 1984's hit duet that [Phil] Collins performed and co-wrote with Philip Bailey. The appearance of 'Easy Lover' … reveals new layers to … the song [which] perfectly spotlights how the killer's delusional megalomania fed his increasingly homicidal behaviour. Criss's ecstatic arm-waving to this frothy pop tune, moving in time with Collins's titanic drum beat, while his prey slowly suffocates, is both chilling and darkly comic. *The Assassination of Gianni Versace* teases out the song's dark subtext and then completely reinvents it. At the scene's climax, Cunanan straddles his would-be customer, raising the scissors above his head. As he plunges the blade into the duct tape covering the man's mouth, finally allowing him to breathe, Collins's screaming vocal lifts on the soundtrack: 'You'll be down on your knees!' Whoa. Was that in 'Easy Lover' from the beginning?

Stephen Hyden, *The Ringer*, June 2018

No Jacket Required

Personnel:
Phil Collins: vocals, drums, keyboards, percussion.
Daryl Stuermer: guitars, keyboards.
David Frank: keyboards on 'Sussudio', 'Don't Lose My Number' and 'Who Said I Would'.
Nick Glennie-Smith: keyboards on We Said Hello Goodbye'.
Leland Sklar: bass guitar.
The Phenix Horns: Rahmlee Michael Davis: trumpet; Michael Harris: trumpet; Don Myrick: saxophone; Louis Satterfield: trombone on 'Sussudio', 'Don't Lose My Number' and 'Who Said I Would'.
Gary Barnacle: saxophone on 'I Don't Wanna Know' and 'Who Said I Would'.

Don Myrick: saxophone on 'One More Night' and 'Inside Out'.
Sting: backing vocals on 'Long Long Way To Go' and 'Take Me Home'.
Peter Gabriel: backing vocals on 'Take Me Home.'
Helen Terry: backing vocals on 'Take Me Home'.
Recorded May–December 1984 at The Townhouse, London and Old Croft, Surrey.
Produced by Phil Collins and Hugh Padgham.
Album release: 11 February 1985.
Highest chart placings: UK; 1; US: 1.
Side one: 'Sussudio', 'Only You Know And I Know', 'Long Long Way To Go', 'I Don't Wanna Know', 'One More Night'
Side two: 'Don't Lose My Number', 'Who Said I Would', 'Doesn't Anybody Stay Together Anymore', 'Inside Out', 'Take Me Home'
Bonus track on CD: 'We Said Hello Goodbye'

'One More Night' b/w **'The Man With The Horn'**
US single release: November 1984. Highest chart position: 1.

'Sussudio' b/w **'The Man With The Horn'**
UK single release: January 1985. Highest chart position: 12.

'One More Night' b/w **'I Like The Way'**
UK single release: April 1985. Highest chart position: 4.

'Sussudio' b/w **'I Like The Way'**
US single release: April 1985. Highest chart position: 1.

'Don't Lose My Number' b/w **'We Said Hello Goodbye'**
US single release: July 1985. Highest chart position: 4.

'Take Me Home' b/w **'We Said Hello Goodbye'**
UK single release: July 1985. Highest chart position: 19.

'Take Me Home' b/w **'Only You Know And I Know'**
US single release: January 1986. Highest chart position: 7.

No Jacket Required is Phil Collins' most commercially successful album. It has sold more than 25 million copies worldwide, was number one in the UK and, for seven weeks, in the US. It was his first solo number one album there. The album also topped the charts in Austria, Canada, Germany, Norway, New Zealand, Spain, Sweden and Switzerland. In his home country, Collins' third solo album would spend 170 weeks in the best-selling lists and was almost permanently resident between March 1985 and October 1987. It won the Grammy for album of the year. However you measure it, *No Jacket Required* was massive.

> The reason why *No Jacket Required* was such a smash is simple: it combined the aching honesty of *Face Value* with the pop smarts of *Hello, I Must Be Going!,* added some seriously focused songwriting, then coated it all in slick digital production that sounded great on the radio. *No Jacket Required* ends up earning all the sales and accolades it got. Collins was at the top of his considerable game, the sound was state of the art, and there were more classic songs on one record than most pop stars could put together in an entire career. Too bad its chart and airwave dominance was so great that it inspired something of a backlash, one Collins never really recovered from despite having more hits in the future.
> Tim Sendra, *Allmusic* review

The album's title was inspired by an incident during the first week of the Robert Plant tour in August 1983. Collins was denied admittance to The Pump Room restaurant in Chicago because he did not meet the restaurant's dress code.

The lead single in the US was 'One More Night', a sparse ballad released several weeks before the parent album. The arrangement is very simple: drum machine, electric piano, guitar and a heartfelt vocal. 'I had a tempo in mind', Collins told *Playboy* in 1986, 'I was thinking of one of the Jacksons' songs, actually – when I strung a chorus on it. The line 'One more night' just fit what I was playing. The rest of the song was written very quickly.'

Don Myrick's sax solo, which plays out the song, adds colour and depth. 'One More Night' was Collins' second US number one single.

In the UK, the more upbeat 'Sussudio' was issued as the first single. Noted for being serial killer Patrick Bateman's favourite Phil Collins song in the novel *American Psycho*, 'Sussudio' bears more than a passing resemblance to Prince's '1999'. Journalist Chris Welch memorably described the song as a 'churning urn of burning funk.'

'It was influenced by Prince, of course,' Phil Collins later admitted, 'and was the first time I worked with dance synth programmers. If anyone thinks I'm ripping off specific songs, that is up to them, but I'm not plagiarizing black music. 'Sussudio' was changed once because it was starting to sound a bit too much like Prince. I could never write a song like Prince because I'm not from that environment.'

The unusual title came from some improvising lyrics. 'I kinda knew I had to find something else for that word,' he said on a 1997 episode of *VH1 Storytellers*. 'This is one of those examples of improvising lyrics. You know, sometimes you can use the lyric, other times you're in big trouble because what you write doesn't mean anything. So I set up this drum-machine pad, and I got some chords, and I started to sing into the microphone, and this word came out, which was 'sus-sussudio.' It just literally came out, at the time. Then I went back and tried to find another word that scanned as well as 'sussudio' and I couldn't find one.'

Only reaching number twelve in the UK, 'Sussudio' provided another US number one in spring 1985. The eleven-minute 12" remix is worth tracking down.

The b-side for 'Don't Lose My Number' and 'Sussudio' is the up-tempo track 'The Man With The Horn', which, like Joni Mitchell's 'For Free', celebrates the humble busker. It features a short, tight saxophone solo by Don Myrick but was inexplicably overlooked when *No Jacket Required* was re-released in 2016. 'The Man With The Horn' was finally collected on 2019's *Other Sides*.

'Don't Lose My Number' followed 'Sussudio' into the US charts in the summer of 1985. It has stabbing guitar, pounding, heavily gated drums and vague, somewhat melodramatic lyrics. Collins himself says there is no real story or message in the song. The MTV-friendly video spoofs the Police, the Cars, *Flashdance,* Elton John (or possibly David Lee Roth) and *The Karate Kid*. 'Don't Lose My Number' was not released as a single in the UK, with preference given to 'Take Me Home'. Unusually, the song was inspired by Ken Kesey's novel *One Flew Over the Cuckoo's Nest* about a patient in a mental hospital ('I've been a prisoner all my life'): the meaning is buried in the video, which shows Collins travelling all over the world during the *No Jacket Required* tour. Both Sting and Phil's former Genesis bandmate Peter Gabriel sing backing vocals on the song, which was performed as the uplifting, valedictory final song at his solo concerts for many years. In 2003 the hip-hop group Bone Thugs-N-Harmony heavily sampled 'Take Me Home'; for their single 'Home'. Their version reached number nineteen in the UK Collins appeared in the video, as he explained in *Rolling Stone*: 'Bone Thugs-N-Harmony called me up and said, 'We've done a version of your song 'Take Me Home' and we'd like you to be in the video.' I said, 'No, I'm not in America.' They said, 'They can come wherever you are.' I said, 'Don't make me say, 'No'. But then I heard the song, and I quite liked it, and they agreed to come to Geneva. How could I disappoint these guys? They were nice lads.'

The hits on *No Jacket Required* are so familiar that it's easy to overlook lesser-heard moments such as 'Inside Out,' 'Long Long Way To Go', 'Only You Know And I Know' and 'Why Doesn't Anybody Stay Together Any More?'

'Inside Out' is a terrific song with an energetic chorus and quieter verses. Don Myrick again contributes a sublime saxophone solo. 'Long Long Way To Go', which features Sting on backing vocals, has a more serious message.

Collins said in *Playboy* in 1986:

> 'Long Long Way To Go' is a political statement. It just doesn't come naturally for me to write like that. I feel that my music is helping in another way – helping people understand more about other people. That's really what I do best. I'm not politically motivated. I don't even vote. I have pretty strong views of what's right and wrong, though. There's so much to do, but for me, that doesn't mean writing political songs. I write personal songs.

'Only You Know And I Know' is a dynamic number which came to life in concert with traded-off guitar and keyboard solos. 'Why Doesn't Anybody Stay Together Any More?' is a weary response to the demise of Eric and Pattie Clapton's marriage, as he later explained to *The Mail on Sunday*: 'All my friends were breaking up with their partners – suddenly it seemed no one wanted to run the distance and work it out. Contrary to what people may think, I tried very hard to work things out with the women who left me. I never took it lying down!'

The spiky 'I Don't Wanna Know' and the anxious 'Who Said I Would' make up the numbers. Finally, the b-side of 'Don't Lose My Number', 'We Said Hello Goodbye', was released as a bonus track on the CD version of *No Jacket Required*. It was not available on the original vinyl or cassette releases. A different mix of the song was released on the soundtrack album to the 1986 film *Playing for Keeps,* where it is listed as 'We Said Hello, Goodbye (Don't Look Back)'. The 2016 re-release of *No Jacket Required* adds demos of 'Only You Know And I Know', 'One More Night' and 'Take Me Home'.

Phil Collins' Commercial Peak

In the last week of March 1985, thirty-four-year-old Phil Collins was at number one in the albums and singles charts simultaneously in both the US and the UK. This was an incredible achievement: only The Beatles (twice, in 1964 and 1966), The Monkees (1967), Simon & Garfunkel (1970), Rod Stewart (1971), Men At Work (1983) and Michael Jackson (1983) had previously achieved this feat.

Even the *New York Times* took notice. Stephen Holden saying on 7 April 1985:

> As both a songwriter and an instrumentalist, Collins is especially adept at sustaining a mood of suspense, often heavily tinged with menace. His shadowy song lyrics are suffused with lurking suspicion, dread and the suggestion of passions so pent-up they could explode violently, though they never do. 'In The Air Tonight', Collins's first major hit, evoked a high gloss horror movie. With drum rolls reminiscent of distant rattling thunder punctuating a hushed, tensed vocal line, one could imagine the singer crouched and sweating in the bushes, ready to confront some unnamed terror. The same waiting-with-bated-breath aura, elevated to an operatic romantic level, also haunted [his] title song for the movie *Against All Odds*. In the process of becoming pop music's master of sophisticated suspense, Collins has forged an odd but powerful mating of English art-rock and American pop-soul. In 1982, his hit version of the Supremes' 1965 hit, 'You Can't Hurry Love', transformed a wistfully ebullient expression of adolescent longing into the slightly creepy *Psycho*-like monologue of a mama's boy. Mr. Collins's latest album contains many echoes of Motown that have been twisted into ambiguous psychological resonances. Collins' astringent voice, with its petulant undertones and grim, wound-up edge is as important as the drums in sustaining a mood of dramatic suspense. And by double-tracking and electronically phasing the vocals, Collins and his producer Hugh Padgham accentuate the sense in his singing of ominous psychological submergence. On the surface, *No Jacket Required* is an album bursting with soulful hooks and bright, peppy tunes. But beneath its shiny exterior, Mr. Collins' drums and his voice carry on a disjunctive, enigmatic dialogue between heart and mind, obsession and repression. The jacket that the album title assures us is not required may not be a tuxedo but a straitjacket.

No Jacket Required, like Dire Straits' *Brothers In Arms* released the same year, was a huge, huge album. But both now seem hermetically sealed in the mid-eighties: it's hard to imagine anyone who wasn't there at the time listening to these albums from beginning to end today.

In the middle of the recording sessions for *No Jacket Required*, Phil Collins married Jill Tavelman, his second wife, at Guildford Registery Office on 4 August 1984. The reception back at Old Croft, including a make-shift party band of Collins, Eric Clapton, Gary Brooker, Mo Foster, Daryl Stuermer, Chester Thompson and Robert Plant.

Band Aid

During sessions at the Townhouse for *No Jacket Required*, Collins received a call from outspoken Boomtown Rats singer Bob Geldof.

Collins: 'I've never met him, but he's straight to the point: 'Did you see the news?' Geldof tells me about Michael Buerk's BBC news report on the famine in Ethiopia. Then he explains his idea for an all-star charity single. 'We have to do something, and I need a famous drummer, and you're the only one I can think of.''

A few days later, Sunday, 25 November 1984, the great and the good of the British music scene convened at Sarm West in Notting Hill – the same studio where Genesis recorded two albums in the early 1970s.

Midge Ure: 'Bob turned up at my place with a guitar that looked as though he'd found it in a dump. It had hardly any strings on it. He started singing me this thing – it was obvious he was making it up as he went along. He sounded like a demented Bob Dylan. There was no melody, no structure and every time he sang it, it sounded different. We wrote the middle section together.'

The basic track was recorded by Ure. Collins came up with a drum part on the spot and recorded it in a single take.

Sting: 'It was a funny day, like a school reunion for truants. All of us had a lot in common but had rarely been in the same room together. There were no fights as I remember.'

Collins said in *Playboy* in October 1986:

> I went to the studio for the session. It was phenomenal. There were about sixty bands there. I think I was the oldest one there. Youch.... So we were all just waiting to do our bit. When it came time for the drums, it was embarrassing because I had the drum kit set up in the middle of the room and everybody was, like, standing there, watching. It took two takes. At the end, everyone stood up and applauded and it was all over so quickly. The best moments happen like that, I think. They mixed it that

> night and the next morning, it was on the radio; the next week, it was number one and the rest is history.

The song went on sale just three days after it was recorded. It remained the UK's biggest-selling single until Elton John's new version of 'Candle in the Wind' overtook it almost fifteen years later.

'Do They Know It's Christmas' closed five astonishing years for Phil Collins. *No Jacket Required* was finished and ready for release. He would soon be everywhere.

Part Two – Staying There

1985

No Jacket Required Tour

The year that kick-started Phil Collins' global success started with the release of *No Jacket Required* on 18 February and a huge, eighty-five date solo tour which took in Europe (February-March), Oceania and Japan (March-April), and North America (May-July).

Phil's band had a slight change this time out, with legendary American bassist Lee Sklar – a veteran of over 2,000 recording sessions – replacing Mo Foster.

The set-list comprised 'I Don't Care Anymore', 'Only You Know And I Know', 'I Cannot Believe It's True', 'This Must Be Love', 'Against All Odds (Take A Look At Me Now)', 'Inside Out', 'Who Said I Would', 'If Leaving Me Is Easy', 'Sussudio', 'Behind The Lines', 'Don't Lose My Number', 'The West Side', 'One More Night', 'In The Air Tonight', 'Like China', 'You Can't Hurry Love', 'It Don't Matter To Me', 'Hand In Hand' and 'Take Me Home'. The encore comprised two songs by The Impressions: 'People Get Ready' and 'It's All Right'.

A few performances have been officially released. 'I Don't Care Anymore' from Melbourne Entertainment Centre on 13 April 1985 can be heard on the deluxe reissue of *Hello, I Must Be Going!*, incorrectly credited there as dating from 1982.

Six songs from the 29 May performance at the Reunion Arena in Dallas have been officially released on the 2016 deluxe reissues of Collins' back catalogue: 'Behind The Lines' on *Face Value*; 'Like China', 'You Can't Hurry Love', 'It Don't Matter To Me' and 'It's Alright' on *Hello, I Must Be Going!*; and 'Who Said I Would' on *...But Seriously*. The entire show was filmed and aired on HBO entitled *No Jacket Required... Sold Out*. The broadcast was later released on VHS and LaserDisc as *Phil Collins: No Ticket Required*.

1985 Academy Awards

Just prior to a series of dates in Australia and Japan, Phil Collins stopped off in Los Angeles to attend the Fifty-Seventh Academy Awards. His song 'Against All Odds (Take A Look At Me Now)' had been nominated for an Oscar.

Despite offering to sing, the producers preferred a horrendous lip-synched interpretative dance by Broadway choreographer Ann Reinking, ex-partner of master choreographer Bob Fosse. Collins sat in the audience, cringing.

'Everyone turns around to look at me, to gauge my reaction. I'm just embarrassed at what she's done to the song. It was awful,' he later said. He's right. This unintentionally hilarious performance can be enjoyed on YouTube.

Stevie Wonder's 'I Just Called To Say I Love You' took the Oscar. 'I'm disappointed that these things aren't necessarily judged on merit,' Collins told *Rolling Stone*. 'Against All Odds (Take A Look At Me Now)' would later win the 1985 Grammy for Best Pop Vocal Performance, Male.

Collins appeared on *The Tonight Show* at around this time, presumably at the end of the tour when he was in New York. He performed 'The Roof Is Leaking'.

Live Aid

> I was in England this afternoon. Funny old world, innit?
> Phil Collins

> The only drawback with Live Aid was that it was the point at which pop music became the establishment, a defining moment when suddenly it developed a conscience. Paradoxically, something died at the same time.
> Tony Banks, *Genesis: Chapter and Verse (2007)*

The Live Aid concerts on 13 July 1985 were notable for Phil Collins performing at both the London and Philadelphia shows. Despite Steve Hackett phoning Tony Banks to regroup with Genesis, the band were never actually asked to take part. 'I never considered whether Genesis could have played,' Collins says in *Genesis: Chapter and Verse*. 'It would have been perfectly logical for me to have played drums in my own band and I'm sure that had it been a moment of activity for Genesis, we would have been asked. But the question never came up.'

Collins initially agreed to perform solo and then to fill the drum seat for his old friend Robert Plant, with whom he had toured a couple of years before.

Collins:

> So I say, breezy as you like, 'I'm sure it'll be OK. [Promoter] Bill [Graham] will be fine!' Then Robert says, 'You, me and Jimmy could do something.'

> The syllables 'Led' and 'Zep' are never uttered. I later find out that they've also asked former Chic drummer Tony Thompson to play, but Robert still wants me on board.

Eric Clapton asks him to sit in. And then Sting calls. 'Are you doing this Geldof concert, Phil?' 'Yeah, I am…' 'Well,' says Sting, 'do you want to do it together?'

A plan is hatched for Collins to appear in London with Sting, then to fly to New York and on to Philadelphia for the American end of the concert. Sting and Collins rehearsed together at Phil's house in West Sussex, working up 'Long Long Way To Go' from *No Jacket Required* and a delightful arrangement of Sting's most famous song, The Police's 'Every Breath You Take'. Sting takes the stage at 3.18 pm to sing 'Roxanne' and 'Driven to Tears' with Collins waiting in the wings. Collins is brought on stage and sits at the piano for the most high-profile performance of his career. 'Good afternoon Wembley' he chirrups, 'good afternoon Philadelphia, good afternoon the world.'

> The stage is white, and it's a very sunny day, so it's blisteringly hot up there. I'm so sweaty that my finger slips off the piano key on 'Against All Odds'. It's a real clanger, and I can almost hear 80,000 people in Wembley wincing. It's the bum note that's heard around the world.

Sting sang his own 'Message In A Bottle' with Collins looking on, then we hear once again, 'In The Air Tonight'. To conclude, they played and sang the wholly appropriate 'Long Long Way To Go' together and an excellent version of 'Every Breath You Take', with wonderful harmonies and spiralling soprano saxophone. It was an impressive set.

Collins boarded a helicopter for the quick hop to Heathrow, where he landed right next to Concorde, which was due to depart on a scheduled trip to New York. Collins tells a hilarious story of meeting Cher:

> During the flight, she comes back to see me. 'Hi, Phil, what's happening?' 'Um, you don't know about this big Live Aid concert? Global jukebox thing, Wembley, Philadelphia, one billion viewers around the world…? We're just on our way to play the American show.' 'Oh,' says Cher. 'Can you get me on it?' I'm thinking, 'What am I, a fucking talent agent?'

Backstage in Philadelphia, having woodshedded the Led Zeppelin songs by listening to his Walkman on Concorde, Collins met Eric Clapton thirty minutes before stepping on stage with his band and learns which songs they'll be performing. He then meets the three ex-members of Led Zeppelin in a tense dressing room.

Collins told *Classic Rock* in 2017:

> I listened to 'Stairway To Heaven' on Concorde. I arrived and went to the caravans, and Robert said: 'Jimmy Page is belligerent.' Page says: 'We've been rehearsing!' And I said: 'I saw your first gig in London; I know the stuff! Jimmy looks at me. 'So,' he says, part drawl, part growl, 'you know what we're playing?' I feel like I've failed a test. What I think Jimmy's actually saying is: 'Do we really need this guy? Do we really need him to be playing with us?' I'm made to feel like the guy who's gate-crashed the party.

Collins performed a three-song, seventeen-minute set with Clapton, then reprised his own two songs from Wembley ('good evening Philadelphia, good evening London, good evening the world'). Despite his 5,700-mile journey between stages, Collins is in fine voice, strong and defined after six months on tour.

The same cannot be said for Robert Plant. At 8.10 pm, Collins joined a very ragged, disjointed Led Zeppelin who were definitely out of practice.

'Robert told me Phil Collins wanted to play with us,' Page explained to *The Scotsman* in 2007. 'I told him that was all right if he knows the numbers. But at the end of the day, he didn't know anything. We played 'Whole Lotta Love', and he was just there bashing away cluelessly and grinning. I thought that was really a joke.'

Collins said in 2017:

> I had a word with [co-drummer] Tony Thompson,' 'I've played as two drummers a lot and it can be a train wreck – and I say: 'Let's stay out of each other's way and play simple.' Thompson, rest his soul, had rehearsed for a week, and I'm about to steal his thunder – the famous drummer's arrived! – and he kind of did what he wanted to do. You can see me miming, playing the air. It was very uncomfortable, and if I could have left that stage, I would have left halfway through 'Stairway…' if not earlier. But imagine the coverage of that? Walking off during The Second Coming? Who the fuck does Collins think he is? Geldof really would have had something to swear about.

This performance was not included in the massive ten-hour, four-DVD box set released in 2004. 'Because, of course, they were ashamed of it,' Collins writes, 'And I find that I am usually the one blamed for it. It couldn't possibly be the holy Led Zep who were at fault. It was that geezer who came over on Concorde who wasn't rehearsed. He was the culprit. That show-off.'

He said in *Playboy*, 1986:

> The only thing that annoyed me was the difference between the American version of Live Aid and the British one. In England, if you wanted a cup of tea, you made it yourself. If you wanted a sandwich, you bought it. In typical American style, at the American concert, there were laminated tour passes and champagne and caviar. I don't doubt anyone's moral commitment to the cause, but the caviar and the cause just didn't jibe for me.

And, after Live Aid 'that show-off' was a global superstar.

'Separate Lives'

'Separate Lives' was written by Phil Collins' friend Stephen Bishop. Bishop sang the song at Collins' wedding reception in 1984.

'Phil really liked my song and wanted me to sing it,' Bishop told Ray Coleman. 'I said: this is a wedding Phil, won't it be kind of weird? And I remember Jill said, go ahead, sing it, it's a good song.'

Collins liked the song enough to record an acoustic version for *No Jacket Required,* but this wouldn't be used on the final album.

Collins recalled in his memoirs:

> But the song hangs around, and eventually Atlantic's Doug Morris calls and says, 'Would you be interested in recording 'Separate Lives' as a duet with Marilyn Martin?' I don't know her, but Doug is president of Atlantic Records, and I trust his judgment. The plan is that the song will be featured in another Taylor Hackford movie, *White Nights*. Here at the height of the Cold War, the world badly needs a ballet/spy mash-up.'

'I was signed to Atlantic records just before Phil turned in his *No Jacket Required* album', Martin told the Kickin' it Old School blog in 2013. 'He had recorded 'Separate Lives' and loved the song, but it didn't seem to fit the rest of his album. When Doug Morris, the label head, heard it, he thought it would make a great duet. To this day, I haven't a clue as to how he convinced Phil to sing it with me, but thank God he did! The first time I met Phil was the night before I was to record my half of the duet. A friend arranged a dinner for us with Phil at Eric Clapton's house... what an amazing night, Phil and his wife, the Claptons, and my friend and me! I was driving on the freeway in L.A. when I first heard ['Separate Lives'] on the radio and it felt so strange, like a dream... it almost didn't register that that was me.'

Despite much promotion from Atlantic, 'Separate Lives' remains Martin's only significant hit. She has since toured as a backing vocalist for Stevie Nicks and for Fleetwood Mac.

'Separate Lives' was released in November 1985, reaching number four in the UK and securing Collins' third chart-topper of the year in the US as well as number one in Ireland and Canada. Bishop recorded his own version for *Sleeping with Girls* and received an Oscar nomination for Best Original Song in 1986.

Press To Play

Shortly after Live Aid, Phil was invited to Paul McCartney's studio, the newly-opened Hog Hill Studios in East Sussex, to play on his album *Press To Play*. Hugh Padham was co-producer. Collins and McCartney were joined by Pete Townshend.

'I'm loath to use the dreaded eighties phrase 'conscience rock', Collins writes, 'but the three of us are switched on, engaged, mature men of the world. We've all been around the block, and around some of the planet's biggest stadiums. Us millionaire musos, we know all about despair, poverty and injustice. We must do. We've all done Live Aid. In the studio, Macca declares, 'When I was doing Live Aid, I felt angry. And I wanted to write a song about it. I felt I should be angry about something. So I wrote this song. It's called 'Angry'.'

'Angry' was completed towards the end of the album's initial batch of recordings in a tight, two-hour Saturday afternoon session. It's full of fire, as you'd expect from a McCartney / Collins / Townshend rhythm section, but lacks lyrical inspiration. Much-delayed, *Press To Play* was released in August 1986.

Collins completists will also need to listen to part fifteen of McCartney's 1995 radio series *Oobu Joobu*, which includes a brief excerpt of a jam recorded with Collins during in the 'Angry' sessions, and find the 12" single of 'Pretty Little Head' which includes a powerful remix of 'Angry' with a horn section and additional orchestration.

Miami Vice

If any TV series embodies the sheen and commercialism of the 1980s then it's NBC's *Miami Vice*. Debuting on 16 September 1984, it used a fast-paced editing style and featured cameos by many famous musicians. A soundtrack album was released after season one, and this included 'In The Air Tonight', putting the song into four million homes. Phil Collins was invited to play the bad guy in the season two episode 'Phil The Shill'.

> It seems that *Miami Vice* wants me to appear in a cameo in one of their episodes. I think it might be a hoot. But when they send me the script, I come out in a cold sweat. Instead of being a cameo, I'm on every page, and in almost every scene. My character is called Phil the Shill. I don't know what a shill is, but it's clear that it's been written with me in mind. I then find out that a 'shill' is a spiv, someone who'll do anything for a buck. I don't know why they thought that was me. I call them and say that I haven't acted in years; I don't know if I can handle this. Director John Nicolella brushes away my concerns. 'Just come over, it'll be fine. We'll have some fun.' So I do, and we do have fun. I'm back home for the summer.

The episode closes with thirty seconds of a unique Phil Collins song: '(Life Is A) Rat Race', a rewrite of the b-side 'The Man With The Horn'.

'Phil the Shill' was broadcast on 13 December 1985. As a follow-up, the song 'Take Me Home', originally released as a single in the UK in July 1985, would be a big hit in the US in March 1986, reaching number seven.

By this time, Collins had recorded Genesis' final and best-selling album of the 1980s.

1986

Invisible Touch

Personnel:
Tony Banks: keyboards, synth bass
Phil Collins: drums, lead vocals, percussion
Mike Rutherford: guitars, bass guitar
Recorded October 1985 – February 1986 at The Farm, Chiddingfold, Surrey.
Produced by Genesis and Hugh Padgham.
Album release: 6 June 1986.
Highest chart placings: UK; 1; US: 1.
Side one: 'Invisible Touch', 'Tonight, Tonight, Tonight', 'Land Of Confusion', 'In Too Deep'
Side two: 'Anything She Does', 'Domino (In The Glow Of The Night / The Last Domino)', 'Throwing It All Away', 'The Brazilian'

'Invisible Touch' b/w 'The Last Domino'

Single release: May 1986. Highest chart position: UK: 15; US: 1.
12" single includes an extended version of 'Invisible Touch'

'In Too Deep' b/w 'Do The Neurotic'

UK single release: August 1986. Highest chart position: 19

'Throwing It All Away' b/w 'Do The Neurotic'

US single release: August 1986. Highest chart position: 4.

'Land Of Confusion' b/w 'Feeding The Fire'

Single release: November 1986. Highest chart position: UK: 14; US: 4.
12" single includes an extended version of 'Land Of Confusion'

'Tonight, Tonight, Tonight' (single edit) b/w 'In The Glow Of The Night'

Single release: February 1987. Highest chart position: UK: 18; US: 3.
12" single includes 'Paperlate' and an extended version of 'Tonight, Tonight, Tonight'

'In Too Deep' b/w 'I'd Rather Be You'

US single release: April 1987. Highest chart position: 3

'Throwing It All Away' b/w 'I'd Rather Be You'

UK single release: June 1987. Highest chart position: 22.
12" single includes a live version of 'Invisible Touch'

> It seemed to me realistic to assume that if you'd got into Genesis in the early days, you probably wouldn't be so keen on *Invisible Touch*. Fans are always going to prefer the era when they first discover you and assume that any change is for the worst. It's a problem common to all long-lived bands. But on stage, when we were playing live, it never felt any different at all to me: it was all a continuum. *Invisible Touch* isn't the definitive Genesis album, but it was probably our hottest moment in terms of commercial success. It was the biggest we would ever get as a band.
> Mike Rutherford, *The Living Years*, 2014

> If ever I was going to quit Genesis in favour of my solo career, in theory, this would be the time, with the tailwind of *No Jacket Required* still blowing hard. But at the same time, I've missed the guys. We go in and improvise. We play. I don't know any other band that works like we do, sitting round, improvising together, until something forms. I think, 'I can't do this anywhere else.' We have something special here.
> Phil Collins, *Not Dead Yet*, 2016

By the summer of 1986, Phil Collins' career was reaching critical mass. In America, he had enjoyed four solo number one singles over the previous two years and, with Genesis, five top five singles since early 1981. His voice, whatever was written on the record sleeve, was now very familiar to radio listeners and record buyers. Furthermore, Mike Rutherford's Mike + The Mechanics had had two huge singles from their debut album, released in the autumn of 1985.

Together, in Genesis, over the next year or so, Collins and Rutherford, with Tony Banks, would achieve colossal commercial success: *Invisible Touch* sold over six million copies in the US, the fourth best-selling album there by a British group in the 1980s. The album spawned five top five hits on the *Billboard* chart – Genesis are the only non-American act to accomplish that feat.

But, by 1986, Genesis sounded very little like the band who had recorded *Seconds Out* ten years before.

'Many older fans blamed Phil Collins and his solo success', writes Steve

Aldous, 'claiming he had changed the band. This view is both incorrect and missing the point. The band's change of direction is something all three members pushed for to challenge themselves musically.'

'You can't mystify people if you want to sell records,' Collins had said in 1985. 'Genesis only began to break [through] when the lyrics became less story-oriented. The basic difference between me and Pete and Tony and Mike is that lyrically they're a bit emotionally screwed up. They went to boarding schools all their lives; only saw their families on holidays, while I went to a regular school; went home every day. They would never put 'I love you' in a lyric, whereas I think nothing of it.'

Genesis' thirteenth studio album was recorded at the band's Farm Studios between October 1985 and February 1986.

'Like *Genesis*, it seemed almost effortless to make,' Mike Rutherford would write in his memoirs. 'My memory of writing it is of going into The Farm and it just flowing. Phil had a little drum machine – a blue, mono Akai – and we'd start with a nothing-very-much loop and jam over it. Phil would sing whatever came into his head and Tony and I would pile in fearlessly with any old chords and noise and racket. And out the songs came.'

The title track and first single opens the album with a blast of major chords. 'Invisible Touch' is one of the most 'pop' songs recorded by Genesis, based around Mike Rutherford's insistent guitar riff and Collins' recurring (and vapid) phrase 'She seems to have an invisible touch, yeah'.

> This is one of my favourite Genesis songs. There was a Sheila E. record out at the time, I think it was 'Glamorous Life', and I wanted to write my own version of that. I had decided to stay in the band even though my solo career had taken off. When you're in a band, it's family. There's the road crew and their families to think about. If you just flippantly say, 'I'm leaving,' they're like, 'We've just bought a house with a mortgage.' You can't do that to people.
>
> Phil Collins, *Rolling Stone*, February 2016

'Invisible Touch' was Genesis' first and only US number one. Perhaps ironically, it was replaced at the top of the charts by Peter Gabriel's 'Sledgehammer' – his only US chart-topping single: he was a pop star, too, in 1986.

A six-minute 12" remix of 'Invisible Touch' reshuffles and repeats various sections, includes a new breakdown section and delivers a cleaner, less-cluttered mix. It is included on the *Archive #2* box set. If 'Uptown Girl', 'Jump', 'Let's Dance', 'Money For Nothing' and 'Dancing In The Dark' unfairly pigeon-hole major rock artists as 1980s pop stars to the wider public, then it's inevitable and unfortunate that we need to add 'Invisible Touch' to that list also.

The follow-up single was 'Throwing It All Away' (in the US) and 'In Too Deep' (in the UK). 'Throwing It All Away' is a simple ballad with Mike Rutherford's sincere lyrics and catchy guitar riff. It's an affecting song which resonated with adult contemporary radio listeners and record buyers – 'Throwing It All Away' reached number four in the US. The minor-key break-up song 'In Too Deep' could be from any of Collins' solo albums. It was written for the much-praised 1986 British film *Mona Lisa* and also plays during a memorable scene in the 2000 film *American Psycho* where the serial killer Patrick Bateman plays the song for two ill-fated prostitutes at his apartment. 'In Too Deep' would not be released as a single in the US until January 1987 to tie in with the band's North American touring schedule. It had been available on *Invisible Touch* for seven months but still reached as high as number three in the Billboard listings.

If it wasn't such a great song, we might argue that 'Land Of Confusion' was almost cynically put together to ring out across huge stadia and radio stations across the world. The message is universal, the rock/pop balance is perfect, and the chorus offers an audience sing-a-long. The single release of 'Land Of Confusion' in November 1986 was accompanied by a memorable video produced by Paul Flattery and directed by Jim Yukich, in which the three members of Genesis were portrayed by puppets from the TV series *Spitting Image*. 'I mentioned to Tony Smith that we should use the puppets,' said Jim Yukich to authors Craig Marks and Rob Tannenbaum in *I Want My MTV* (2011). 'Each puppet cost $10,000 to make. Not just the Genesis puppets but [all the others].'

'I've done twenty-three videos for Phil Collins and about fifteen for Genesis,' Flattery told Marks and Tannenbaum. 'We never once had a contract between us. Just a handshake agreement on the budget. They never, ever stinted. Which didn't mean they didn't complain. If you look at 'Land Of Confusion', which is their favourite video because they didn't have to be in it, you'll notice Tony Banks playing a cash register. That's because he was always complaining about how much videos cost.' Collins still has one of the puppets.

'Land Of Confusion' won a Grammy for Best Concept Music Video. This remains Genesis' only Grammy award: for a video in which they do not appear. The 12" mix extends the song to seven minutes.

The coolly anthemic 'Tonight, Tonight, Tonight' is perhaps the quintessential late 80s Genesis song – equal parts catchy and experimental: 50% pop, 50% prog. Like 'Land Of Confusion', it sounded great blasting across the stadiums of Europe, Oceania and North America in 1986-1987. 'Tonight, Tonight, Tonight' appears to takes its main riff from 'The Big Sky' by Kate Bush, released in September 1985, just as Genesis were coming together to write *Invisible Touch*. This might be merely coincidence, but the similarities are surprising. There are two alternative mixes for completists. The single release is heavily edited – the introduction has 17 seconds snipped out and the sections between 2.55 – 5.06 and 6.00 – 7.46 have been removed. The extended 12" version is 11.47 and includes both a two-minute introduction and longer fade-out with a fuller guitar solo.

The confident, colossal 'Domino' is quintessential Tony Banks and classic Genesis. The lyrics don't flow – they were inspired by the conflict in Lebanon between 1982 and 1985 – but somehow, Collins makes them work.

> Sheets of double glazing help to keep outside the night / Only foreign city sirens can cut through
> Nylon sheets and blankets help to minimize the cold / But they can't keep out the chilling sounds

'They're not the kind of lyrics that I would write,' Collins said in *Chapter and Verse*, 'but I realized, 'I can find it, I can see it now, I can do it.' And that was a pleasant surprise.'

'Domino', with its challenging theme, melodic invention, dramatic shifts and driving energy is a progressive rock masterpiece – an eleven-minute song full of tension and anxiety that somehow found its way into millions of pop fans' homes. 'Domino' matured into another song altogether in concert and has been the centrepiece of all full-length Genesis shows since 1986 – even those with Ray Wilson replacing Collins.

> By 1986, Collins had become one of the world's biggest stars, as the soul-rock confections of his solo albums led him to multi-platinum success and a budding movie career. Much of that year's Genesis album *Invisible*

> *Touch* – its bright, polished pop title track, the baby boomer agit-rock of 'Land Of Confusion', the genuinely affecting ballad 'Throwing It All Away' – could have easily fitted on his solo albums. 'Domino', however, was different. This track is a fusion of everything Genesis had ever been and now become: an eleven-minute multi-part epic played with the minimal attack of 'Abacab', the haunting 'In The Glow Of The Night' giving way to the anthemic synth-rock bombast of 'The Last Domino'... a final gasp of brilliance before the blandness of 1991's *We Can't Dance* and 1997's inexplicable, Collins-less *Calling All Stations*.
> Stevie Chick, *The Guardian*, 2014

'Anything She Does' is a brassy retread of 'Illegal Alien' and 'Paperlate': fast and unsubtle. It was the only song from *Invisible Touch* not performed on the subsequent tour – instead, a video by Flattery and Yukich would be used as an introduction to live performances. The closing track, the atmospheric electro-synth 'The Brazilian', was nominated for Best Pop Instrumental Performance (Orchestra, Group Or Soloist) at the 1986 Grammies. It lost to the theme from *Top Gun* by Harold Faltermeyer.

There are three b-sides available. 'Do The Neurotic', the b-side of 'In Too Deep' in the UK and 'Throwing It All Away' in the US, is a lengthy instrumental which fails to engage. A longer version can be heard on both *Archive #2* (2000) and the *Extra Tracks* CD included with the *1983-1998* box set (2009). 'Feeding The Fire', the b-side of 'Land Of Confusion' could be a track from *A Trick Of The Tail*. As with the b-sides 'Submarine' and 'Naminanu', Genesis seemed to shy away from any tracks that hark back too far into their own history. The unrelentingly upbeat 'I'd Rather Be You' was released as the b-side of 'In Too Deep' (US) and 'Throwing It All Away' (UK). This is pure Motown with a Genesis twist.

'No One Is To Blame'

'No One Is To Blame' was British musician Howard Jones' ninth single: six of these reached the top ten in Britain between 1983 and 1985. 'No One Is To Blame' was first released on the album *Dream In Action*; the song was tagged as a potential single, a follow-up to his biggest American hit so far, the bittersweet and almost-forgotten 'Things Can Only Get Better'.

Phil Collins was invited to produce a new version with Hugh Padgham; he is prominent on drums and backing vocals. Recorded at The Farm in late 1985 with Mo Foster (bass) and Phil Palmer (guitar), the single was released in March 1986 and reached number 4 in the US – Jones' biggest hit – and number 16 in the UK.

Sessions for Eric Clapton, Phil Bailey, Chaka Khan and Tina Turner

Between the completion of the recording of *Invisible Touch* and the start of the tour some months later, Phil Collins kept busy, as usual. In April and May 1986, he co-produced Eric Clapton's album *August* in Los Angeles. Songs written in this period, such as 'Tearing Us Apart', 'Take A Chance' and 'Holy Mother' reflect different aspects of Clapton's complicated life. Eric Clapton's tenth solo album is unlike any other album in his back catalogue: it's a bright-sounding and very commercial album which consists mostly, of lightweight soul/pop songs, polished with a production sheen that relegates Clapton's singing and playing to the back of the mix. It is only on the mercurial 'Holy Mother' – the best song here by a long way – and on grittier songs such as 'Hung Up On Your Love', 'Miss You' and the b-side 'Wanna Make Love To You' that the real Clapton emerges. *August* was released on 24 August 1986: a top three album with certified Platinum sales and a forty-six-week chart run. The core band for these sessions – Clapton, Collins, Greg Phillinganes and Nathan East – undertook a short tour of festivals in Europe in July 1986, followed by two nights at the National Exhibition Centre in Birmingham.

At these shows, Collins sang what could be the definitive version of 'that song', evidenced by the hour-long special broadcast on *The Tube* in December 1986 and released on the *Eric Clapton and Friends – Live 1986* DVD.

The Collins-East rhythm section had previously worked together on two tracks on Philip Bailey's guest-laden album *Inside Out*, released in spring 1986. Both musicians are credited as co-writers on 'Because Of You' and 'Back It Up', along with keyboardist George Duke and guitarist Ray Parker Jr. 'Because of You', a slick soul ballad, features vocalist and co-writer Lorelei McBroom; the energetic 'Back It Up' has contributions from producer and co-writer Nile Rogers and the transcendent Jeff Beck.

'Watching the World' is a powerful track from Chaka Khan's sixth album, *Destiny* released in June 1986. Collins drums and adds his distinctive backing vocals to a song written for Khan by Richard Page, Steve George and John Lang of Mr. Mister. There is an extended 12" remix of this track if you want to collect everything.

Destiny was a play for Tina Turner's rock/pop audience and, true to form, Collins plays on two tracks on *Break Every Rule*, Turner's follow-up to her globally successful *Private Dancer*. 'Typical Male' is characteristic of Turner's mid-80s sound and has many trademark Collins fills. It reached number two on the *Billboard* listings. 'Girls', meanwhile, is a little-known David Bowie song which starts slowly and builds to a big chorus with those gated drums right out front. *Break Every Rule* was released in September 1986.

Amidst all of this, Collins was once again part of the house band for the annual Prince's Trust Rock Gala, this time held at Wembley Arena on 20 June 1986. He sang – guess what? – 'In The Air Tonight' and held down the drum stool for performances by some familiar names: Tina Turner, Eric Clapton (the Collins-produced 'Tearing Us Apart'), Mark Knopfler, Howard Jones (the Collins-produced 'No One Is To Blame'), Rod Stewart, Elton John, Midge Ure, Joan Armatrading, Paul Young, George Michael and Paul McCartney (who declined to perform 'Angry').

Invisible Touch Tour

The first leg of the massive ten-month, 112 date *Invisible Touch* tour included large arenas and stadiums across the US, Canada, New Zealand and Australia between September and December 1986. The set included most of *Invisible Touch* and comprised 'Mama', 'Abacab', 'Land Of Confusion', 'That's All', 'Domino (In The Glow Of The Night –The Last Domino)', 'In Too Deep', 'The Brazilian', 'Follow You Follow Me', 'Tonight, Tonight, Tonight', 'Home By The Sea / Second Home By The Sea', 'Throwing It All Away', the 'old medley' of 'In The Cage', '...In That Quiet Earth' and the 'Apocalypse in 9/8' and 'As Sure As Eggs Is Eggs' sections of 'Supper's Ready', then 'Invisible Touch', 'Drum Duet' and 'Los Endos' with 'Turn It On Again' complete with snippets of oldies as the encore.

A live version of 'In Too Deep' from The Forum, Los Angeles, is on the 'I Can't Dance' CD single (1991) and *The Way We Walk The Shorts* (1992). Both 'Throwing It All Away' and 'Invisible Touch' from these dates were added to the 12" single release of 'Throwing It All Away', released in June 1987. A magnificent version of 'Your Own Special Way' with an eight-piece string section was performed at the Australian shows, and a recording from the Sydney Entertainment Centre in December 1986 is available on the 'Hold On My Heart' CD single (1992) and on the *Archive #2* box set (2000). A recording of 'That's All' from this tour is included in the 1992 CD single release of 'I Can't Dance'.

The Playboy Interview

Collins was interviewed at length by David Scheff for the October 1986 edition of the long-running lifestyle magazine *Playboy*.

DS: Phil, we've all heard the rumours; are they true?
PC: You mean about me----
DS: Yes. About your being the so-called nicest person in rock 'n' roll.
PC: Well, it's true that I always end up apologizing for being a nice guy. I don't understand why I have to. I do interviews and then the writers come back and say, 'My editor doesn't believe you're like this and he wants more to make the story better.' Like what? Sex? Drugs? Sorry. This is me. A writer in England went up to my mom and asked her what my faults were. She said, 'I can't think of any of his faults.' So the headline was: 'Faultless Phil. Mr. Perfect, by his Mom.' She read it and went berserk. She doesn't need that at 73.
DS: Then it's not true? You deny the charges?
PC: I'm nice until I have a reason not to be. I work hard and people sense that. But I'm different things to different people. To the middle-aged housewife, I'm someone who looks like a 'little boy lost'; to the people who know only 'One More Night' and 'Against All Odds (Take A Look At Me Now)', I'm probably this sweet and sensitive guy. But there are many other songs, many other sides. I don't like that sickly sweet image.
DS: Critics have been tough on you for not having enough of an edge. How do you react to bad reviews?
PC: If you don't want to believe the bad ones, then you can't believe the good ones, but I don't have to accept the critics who obviously just don't like me. Robert Hilburn [of the *Los Angeles Times*] just doesn't like me. He wrote a review of 'One More Night', complaining about how many times I use the line 'One more night' in the song. How many times does Bruce Springsteen say 'Born in the USA' in 'Born in the USA'? Well, Hilburn is a huge Springsteen fan. And the point is irrelevant. There was a whole page of letters in the paper from his own readers angry with him. Anyway, some critics just respond to ballads and love songs. They think it's a little soppy to write about those things. But the stuff that really gets me is the comments about my physical appearance. I guess it's easier to write about than the kind of songs I play. I mean, I was called the ugliest man since George Orwell. What's that got to do with the music? And, by the way, how ugly was George Orwell?
DS: *Rolling Stone* called you a 'Cabbage Patch Kid for the pop audience.'

PC: Yes, and after that came out, people started to throw Cabbage Patch dolls onto the stage. Listen: I'm gonna clear up a few things here: One, I'm not short. People keep saying I am short. I'm 5'8', which in England is the average height, OK? Two, I'm not bald. They all talk about the balding rock star. I have had this hairline since I was a kid, right? Of course, I am losing it gradually, but I started off with less than everybody else. Three, I'm only a little bit overweight, and that's because I have lived in the studio for the past six months and studio work is tedious. There is a lot of sitting around. I get fit on the road. I lose a lot of excess pounds when I'm on stage. On this tour with Genesis, since I'm playing drums more than when I tour myself, I really burn a lot of calories. So there. That's cleared up. But I understand the point. The traditional pop star is more glamorous. Lifestyle, clothes, a bit of arrogance. I'm not going to apologize for not being like that.

1987

Second and Third Legs of Invisible Touch Tour

The second leg of the Genesis tour covered six weeks in the US between mid-January and early March 1987, and then a series of dates in Japan.

With the rest of the band taking a six-week break, Collins undertook another thirteen-date tour with Eric Clapton, a reprise of the Clapton/Collins/Phillinganes/East dates from the previous summer, with the same set-list and support act. The final dates in Providence and New York City were recorded for a proposed live album. So far, these recordings are (officially) unreleased.

On 15 April, both Clapton and Collins appeared at the Ebony Showcase Theater in Los Angeles for television special *A Blues Session* with B.B. King, broadcast on HBO / Cinemax. King duetted with the likes of Gladys Knight, Billy Ocean, Chaka Khan, Stevie Ray Vaughan, Albert King, Paul Butterfield and Etta James. Clapton, Collins and Butterfield added instrumentation to King's signature tune, 'The Thrill Is Gone'. They also play along in a ramshackle group performance of 'Let The Good Times Roll'.

Genesis regrouped for a long series of massive stadium gigs in southern Europe, the US, and northern Europe between mid-May and early July. Your author attended the massive (and very wet) gig at Roundhay Park in Leeds on 28 June – I was unimpressed at the time, as anyone sitting alone for six hours in a wet field might be. But recordings prove that they were outstanding that night. The tour culminated in four consecutive concerts at Wembley Stadium in London, 1-4 July 1987.

The set was more or less the same as the 1986 shows, but 'Follow You Follow Me' and 'In Too Deep' were dropped and the voice-stretching extract from 'Supper's Ready' was replaced by '...In That Quiet Earth' and 'Afterglow'.

> Nearly 300,000 people [over four nights] at Wembley. I thought at the time, and I still think now, that moment was the peak of our career.
> Tony Banks, *Genesis: Chapter and Verse* (2007)

Collins wrote later:

> Wembley is tremendously atmospheric, and the four nights we play there are easily the triumph of the tour. When you're onstage in front of 86,000

> people—at the legendary home of English football—and you lead them in lovely, daft crowd antics ('woo-ooo' when the lights come down during my introduction to 'Domino,' for example), it's a thrilling, intoxicating sight. I feel very powerful that night. Top of the world, Ma.

The video *Invisible Touch Tour* was released in 1988. This was re-released in 2003, and renamed *Genesis Live at Wembley Stadium*. Several audio tracks from these shows have been made available over the years. 'Domino' was included as a CD single with some editions of the *Invisible Touch Tour* video. An 8.37 edited version of 'Abacab' was the b-side of the 1992 live single of 'Invisible Touch', Genesis' last top ten hit in the UK. The CD single includes the full-length 'Abacab' and adds 'The Brazilian' from these shows. The latter can also be heard on *Archive #2* (2000). 'Mama' and 'That's All' are on *The Way We Walk – The Shorts* (1992). 'Invisible Touch' and 'Tonight, Tonight, Tonight' from 4 July are on the CD singles 'No Son Of Mine' (1992) and 'Tell Me Why' (1993), respectively.

Buster Is Announced

Around the time of the first European dates of the tour in mid-May, Collins flew to the Cannes Film Festival to announce that we was to star in the film *Buster*. He said that was keen to return to acting as he liked the idea of a romantic comedy and because Julie Walters also agreed to be involved.

> I did *Buster* because I loved the story. I loved the script and I wanted to act. It was a great vehicle for me.
> Phil Collins, WEA promo interview, 1989

'I do wake up some mornings in a cold sweat. I mean, I was only a kid when I acted before,' he told Michael Watts when interviewed for *Options For Men* in May 1988. 'I don't think I could be somebody else if [wife Jill] was around. And Julie's playing my wife, after all. I'll have to flirt. Jill's already asked if there are any 'bits' in it. I've told her not really, not at the moment.'

David Green, the film's director, had no hesitation in choosing Phil for the role. 'I'd seen his performance in *Miami Vice* and was bowled over,' he told Watts. 'He's perfect for the character of Buster, similar in both age and looks. But more than that, he's a genuinely warm family man, happy go lucky and with a great sense of humour.'

The film would go into production in early 1988.

As a potential movie star, Phil Collins held all the aces. He had looks, of proven appeal to women, he could sing and he could act.
Ray Coleman, *Phil Collins The Definitive Biography*, 1997

Prince's Trust Rock Gala 1987

Collins was somehow able to fit in an appearance at the second of two Prince's Trust concerts in London on a night off between Genesis gigs in Denmark and Germany. He sang an energetic medley of Four Tops songs as a duet with Paul Young (the Luton-born 'blue-eyed soul' singer, not the Mechanic). Young was touring as Genesis' support act at the time.

Unlike previous shows in the series, Collins didn't sit in with the house band for the duration of the concert, but he did commandeer Ray Cooper's kit for the shambolic finale of 'With A Little Help From My Friends'. Collins is credited online as appearing on both nights – 5 and 6 June 1987 – but he was on stage with Genesis at the Gentofte Stadion in Copenhagen on the first of these dates.

Highlights from the show(s) were released as an album and video in 1988.

12"ers

The 12" remix had emerged in the late 1970s, allowing longer versions of songs to be available to consumers and DJs. Donna Summer's 'Love To Love You Baby' is extended to almost seventeen minutes on her groundbreaking 1975 single. The addition of longer, extended, or remixed versions of songs on the 12" format brought record companies additional sales, even if the end results often diluted the effect of the original.

Phil Collins released 12" mixes of his four singles from *No Jacket Required*: 'Don't Lose My Number', 'Take Me Home', 'Sussudio' and 'One More Night'. A long edit of 'Only You Know And I Know' was released as the B-side of the 'Separate Lives' 12" single.

All of these were collected together on this October 1987 album, along with an extended version of 'Who Said I Would', which was made available for the first time.

Thirty-two years later, Collins released the digital album *Remixed Sides* (May 2019), which includes these six tracks and twelve other extended remixes. From Collins' 1980s output, we have the 1988 Ben Liebrand remix of 'In The Air Tonight' along with its extended version;

the extended dance mix of 'Easy Lover' (also available on the 2011 rerelease of *Chinese Wall*); Nicka's Stella Polaris interpretation of 'The Roof Is Leaking'; a new 'medley mega mix' of 'Sussudio', 'Don't Lose My Number' and 'You Can't Hurry Love'; the 'One World' remix of 'Something Happened On The Way To Heaven'; and no less than four remixes of 'Hang In Long Enough'. Only the most rabid collectors need to track this collection down.

1988

Buster

Phil Collins spent the first few months of 1988 filming *Buster* on location in London (Temple, Embankment, Westminster, Bethnal Green, Harlesden, West Norwood, Barnet, Brixton, Clapton and Kingsbury Green), Rickmansworth, Pinner, Weybridge, at the Great Central Railway in Loughborough and in Acapulco, Mexico.

Buster was written by Colin Schindler and directed by David Green, who had earned his spurs helming *Emmerdale Farm* and *Whicker's World*. Collins is joined by the cream of British acting talent, including Julie Walters, Larry Lamb, Michael Attwell, Ralph Brown, Sheila Hancock and Martin Jarvis. *Halliwell's Film Guide* describes the film as an 'uneasy combination of romantic comedy and chase thriller'.

It's Only Rock And Roll

The Atlantic Records' 40th Anniversary Concert – dubbed 'It's Only Rock And Roll' – was a thirteen-hour televised concert held at Madison Square Garden on 14 May 1988. It was Collins' only live show between July 1987 and August 1989.

The performers were, in order: The Coasters, Phil Collins (singing 'that song' again), LaVern Baker, Foreigner, Iron Butterfly, Laura Branigan, Ben E. King, Roberta Flack with Peabo Bryson, Crosby, Stills & Nash, The Bee Gees, Emerson and Palmer (without Lake), Yes, The Rascals, Vanilla Fudge, Average White Band, Ruth Brown, Debbie Gibson, Robert Plant, The Manhattan Transfer, The (Detroit) Spinners, The MGs with Carla Thomas, Paul Rodgers, Miki Howard, Dan Aykroyd and Sam Moore with Phil Collins and Wilson Pickett (Collins joins Aykroyd and Moore to sing 'You Don't Know Like I Know' and 'Knock on Wood'), Bob Geldof, Genesis and Rufus Thomas.

The concert ended with a thirty-minute set from a reunited Led Zeppelin with Jason Bonham on drums. Whilst the Led Zep performance was a significant improvement on Live Aid three years before, it was still shaky at times. Collins was not invited to sit in.

Genesis extended their in-concert arrangement of 'Turn It On Again' to include 'Land Of Confusion', 'Misunderstanding', 'Throwing It All Away', 'You Can't Hurry Love' (the only time that Genesis would perform Collins' 1982 solo hit), 'Shortcut To Somewhere' (from Banks' 1986 album *Soundtracks*), 'All I Need Is A Miracle' (Mike + The Mechanics' 1985 hit), 'That's All', 'Tonight, Tonight, Tonight', and 'Invisible Touch'. The performance is professional but not inspired. Collins reads some of the lyrics from cue cards.

He finally met American singer David Crosby at this event. After wanting to work with Crosby for some time, Collins was able to invite him to contribute to the forthcoming Los Angeles recording sessions for *...But Seriously*.

Boys Don't Cry

In the 1980s, Collins' ex-Flaming Youth bandmate Brian Chatton was in a band called Boys Don't Cry. Their biggest hit was the cheesy and faintly racist novelty song 'I Wanna Be A Cowboy'. Collins was explicitly credited on the June 1988 Boys Don't Cry single 'We Got The Magic'. This insipid power ballad failed to chart anywhere, despite Collins' name being prominently featured on the sleeve and label. He also appeared in the video, which is hilariously awful.

Buster Soundtrack

The single 'A Groovy Kind Of Love' was Phil Collins' first new music as a solo artist since 'Separate Lives', three years before.

> I say, 'We need a love song from that period somewhere, something Buster and June might hear on the radio—a crooner like Andy Williams singing a ballad like, say, 'A Groovy Kind of Love.'' 'Great idea, Phil!' 'Yeah, but not me,' I clarify, panicked. 'OK, but can you give us a demo of it, so we know what you mean?' I call Tony Banks and ask him for the chords of the song, record a quick half-hour demo version, then send it to the producers. 'This is fantastic, Phil!' 'But you'll get someone else to sing it, right?' 'Sure we will.' I go to see a rough cut of the film and there it is, my demo, playing over a romantic goodbye kiss between Julie and me. I protest. But because it works so well in the film, I'm stuck with it. So we re-record 'A Groovy Kind of Love,' with orchestral maestro Anne Dudley producing, and that version is released as a single.

Such was Collins' popularity that the very dull 'A Groovy Kind Of Love' was number one in both the UK and the US.

Three other new songs were included on the soundtrack. Two of these were co-written by Collins with legendary Motown songwriter and producer Lamont Dozier.

> Lamont Dozier came backstage in L.A. and we exchanged love and phone numbers, and vows to work together. He agrees to write some songs. He flies to Acapulco, where we're filming scenes from Buster's exile, bringing with him a couple of musical sketches: an instrumental with a title, 'Loco in Acapulco,' but no lyrics, and another piece which has neither title nor lyrics. Overnight I write the lyrics to both, give the second a title, 'Two Hearts,' then go up to Lamont's hotel room and sing them to him. 'Well,' Lamont says, smiling, 'you're going to have to sing them now, they're your songs…' As it's to be placed in the middle of the film, I refuse to sing 'Loco in Acapulco.' I eventually ask The Four Tops and produce them with Lamont. I have the unnerving job of singing the melody to Levi Stubbs, one of the most incredible voices of the sixties. I come under heavy pressure, however, to sing 'Two Hearts.' Eventually, I say, 'OK, but it's not going to be before the end credits, is it? I want people to decide whether I can act before they hear me singing.'

'Two Hearts', pure Motown with an 80s spin, was released as the follow-up to 'A Groovy Kind Of Love'. It was Collins' sixth solo number one in the US, and a number six in the UK. 'Loco In Acapulco', with Collins on drums, reached number seven in the UK but failed to chart in America.

The infectious 'Big Noise' is a terrific homage to Phil's love of soul music and is available only on the *Buster* soundtrack. It, too, would have been a huge hit single.

Buster received a Royal Premiere at the Odeon, Leicester Square on 15 September 1988, in aid of The Prince's Trust. The soundtrack album was released that same month. It's testament to Collins' massive popularity that the album reached number six in the UK

'Two Hearts' earned a Grammy Award for Best Song Written Specifically for a Motion Picture or Television in 1989, a Golden Globe Award for Best Original Song (tying with 'Let The River Run' from *Working Girl* by Carly Simon) and an Academy Award nomination for Best Original Song.

The Living Years

If Phil Collins' solo success as a pop artist came as a surprise, then Mike Rutherford's was perhaps more so. Whilst not pin-up material (nor a singer of particular note), Rutherford had, it must be remembered, written the melodies, chord structures and lyrics of four of Genesis' biggest hits: 'Follow You Follow Me', 'Turn It On Again', 'Land Of Confusion' and 'Throwing It All Away'. Forming the ad hoc band Mike +

The Mechanics was a side project with unexpected benefits – Rutherford could sit back in a group context and not worry about being the sole focus.

The Mechanics' self-titled debut album provided two *Billboard* top ten hits. Their second album, *The Living Years*, recorded whilst Phil Collins was filming *Buster*, included the title track which was a US number one and UK number two when released as single in 1989.

Rutherford's Genesis bandmates made a half-hidden guest appearance on *The Living Years*. The track 'Black & Blue' includes a sample by Banks of Collins and Rutherford playing a riff during the *Invisible Touch* sessions. This provides the basis of the song's backing track. Vocalist Paul Young sings brilliantly.

1989

Bowling In Paris, Seeds Of Love and Journeyman

Collins produced four tracks on Stephen Bishop's 1989 album *Bowling in Paris*. The atmospheric 'Sleeping With Girls' features Randy Crawford and Brenda Russell on backing vocals and Nathan East on bass. Collins also brings out Bishop's inner rocker in the muscular 'Love At A Distance', which utilises the skills of Mo Foster on bass, former Flaming Youth Ronnie Caryl on guitar and Adrian Lee from Mike + The Mechanics on keyboards. The lively drums suggest the Townhouse as the recording venue. Lee, Foster and Caryl also appears on the very commercial 'Walking On Air', a re-recording of the closing theme to the 1986 film *The Boy Who Could Fly*. Both Sting and Eric Clapton guest on the album's final track, 'Hall Light', lightweight AOR which was recorded in spring 1984 amid sessions for Clapton's *Behind The Sun* album. Phil Collins plays drums on all four of the above, as well as singing some backing vocals. The album boasts a thank you in the liner notes to Nintendo 'for the brain rest via Super Mario II and Solomon's Key'.

British pop duo Tears For Fears displayed a new maturity with the release of their third album *Seeds Of Love*, in September 1989. Collins provides the drums on the opening track, 'Woman In Chains'.

> When I did that Tears For Fears song, they said, 'This is where we want the big drum fill.' And straight away, I knew what they meant. I said, 'I've done that. I can't do the son of Da-Da, Da-Da, Da-Da. I can do something, but I can't do that.' And I felt they were disappointed that they didn't get what they had hoped for.
>
> Phil Collins, *Plays Well With Others* sleevenotes, 2018

Listen to the album version at 3:32 when Collins's drums come in – it's easy to hear how an 'In The Air Tonight' drum roll would have fitted into the band's ideas for the arrangement. Collins keeps it simple but slips in a more complex variant of his famous drum fill at 4:35. Due reverence should be paid here to Curt Smith's lyrical bass playing and to the terrific lead vocals by Roland Orzabal and Oleta Adams. *Seeds Of Love* was a major hit – another number one album in Phil Collins' discography.

Eric Clapton's 'Bad Love' was recorded at the Townhouse in June 1989 for the album *Journeyman*, released the following November. Pino Palladino's liquid fretless bass introduces a furious guitar riff copped straight from 'Layla', arpeggios from 'Badge' and Phil Collins' thundering drums. Clapton remembered in his memoirs how the song came about:

> Warner Bros. wanted another 'Layla'. I thought, well, if you sit down and write a song in a formatted way, it's not so hard. You think, 'What was 'Layla' comprised of? A fiery intro modulated into the first verse and chorus with a riff around it. I had this stuff in my head, so I just juggled it around, and Mick Jones [of Foreigner] came in to help tidy up. He was the one who said, 'You should put a 'Badge' middle in there'. So, we did that. Although it sounds like a cold way of doing it, it actually took on its own life.

'Layla' it ain't, despite a guitar solo that flies above the bridge. 'Bad Love' won the award for Best Rock Vocal Performance, Male at the 33rd Annual Grammy Awards in 1990.

In the midst of all this activity, Collins became a father for the third time when his wife Jill gave birth to their daughter Lily on 18 March 1989.

...But Seriously

Personnel:
Phil Collins: vocals, keyboards, drums, percussion
Daryl Stuermer: guitar on 'Hang In Long Enough', 'That's Just The Way It Is', 'Do You Remember?', 'Something Happened On The Way To Heaven', 'Heat On The Street', 'Father To Son' and 'Find A Way To My Heart'
Dominic Miller: guitar on 'Hang In Long Enough', 'Something Happened On The Way To Heaven', 'Colours', 'Another Day In Paradise' and 'All Of My Life'
Eric Clapton: guitar on 'I Wish It Would Rain Down'
Nathan East: bass on 'Hang In Long Enough' and 'Something Happened On The Way To Heaven'
Leland Sklar: bass on 'That's Just The Way It Is', 'Colours', 'Another Day In Paradise', 'Heat On The Street', 'All Of My Life', 'Saturday Night and Sunday Morning', 'Father To Son' and 'Find A Way To My Heart'
Pino Palladino: bass on 'Do You Remember?' and 'I Wish It Would Rain Down'
The Phenix Horns: Don Myrick: saxophone; Louis Satterfield: trombone; Harry Kim: trumpet; Rhamlee Michael Davis: trumpet on 'Hang In Long Enough', 'Something Happened On The Way To Heaven', 'Colours', 'All Of My Life', 'Saturday Night and Sunday Morning' and 'Find A Way To My Heart'
Steve Winwood: Hammond organ on 'All Of My Life'
Alex Brown, Marva King and Lynne Fiddmont: backing vocals on 'Hang In Long Enough', 'Something Happened On The Way To Heaven', 'Heat On The

Street' and 'All Of My Life'
David Crosby: vocals on 'That's Just The Way It Is' and 'Another Day In Paradise'
Stephen Bishop: vocals on 'Do You Remember?'
Recorded April–October 1989 at The Farm, Chiddingfold, Surrey and A&M Studios, Los Angeles.
Produced by Phil Collins and Hugh Padgham.
Album release: 7 November 1989
Highest chart placings: UK; 1; US: 1.
LP side one: 'Hang In Long Enough', 'That's Just The Way It Is', 'Find A Way To My Heart', 'Colours', 'Father To Son'
LP side two: 'Another Day In Paradise', 'All Of My Life', 'Something Happened On The Way To Heaven', 'Do You Remember?', 'I Wish It Would Rain Down'
CD: 'Hang In Long Enough', 'That's Just The Way It Is', 'Do You Remember?', 'Something Happened On The Way To Heaven', 'Colours', 'I Wish It Would Rain Down', 'Another Day In Paradise', 'Heat On The Street', 'All Of My Life', 'Saturday Night and Sunday Morning', 'Father To Son', 'Find A Way To My Heart'

'Another Day In Paradise' b/w 'Heat On The Street', 'Saturday Night and Sunday Morning'

Single release: October 1989. Highest chart position: UK: 2; US: 1.

'I Wish It Would Rain Down' b/w 'Homeless'

UK single release: January 1990. Highest chart position: 7

'I Wish It Would Rain Down' b/w 'You've Been in Love (That Little Bit Too Long)'

US single release: January 1990. Highest chart position: 3

'Something Happened On The Way To Heaven' b/w 'I Wish It Would Rain Down' (Demo)

UK single release: April 1990. Highest chart position: 15.

'Do You Remember?' b/w 'I Wish It Would Rain Down' (Demo)

US single release: April 1990. Highest chart position: 4.

'That's Just The Way It Is' b/w 'Broadway Chorus'

UK single release: July 1990. Highest chart position: 26.

'Something Happened On The Way To Heaven' b/w 'I Wish It Would Rain Down' (Demo)

US single release: July 1990. Highest chart position: 4.

'Hang In Long Enough' b/w 'Around The World In 80 Presets'

UK single release: September 1990. Highest chart position: 34.

'Hang In Long Enough' b/w 'Separate Lives' (live)

US single release: October 1990. Highest chart position: 23.

> My 1989 album ...*But Seriously* has that title for a couple of reasons. For one thing, on March 18 that year, Jill gives birth to our daughter Lily. I'm suddenly enveloped all over again in feelings of parental responsibility and doting fatherhood. I'm looking inward at my family, but I'm also looking outward at the world in which Lily will grow up. These thoughts are mirrored in the songs I've been writing: socially and politically engaged songs about, respectively, the homeless, apartheid, the Troubles in Northern Ireland and inner-city unrest. You can divine my state of mind by my expression on the cover art, which, as ever, features nothing more than my face. I'm wearing my heart, and my seriousness, on my album sleeve.

Unlike Phil Collins' first three solo albums, ... *But Seriously* features some high-profile guests. Eric Clapton, Steve Winwood and Stephen Bishop add their skills to three songs. David Crosby plays a major part in 'That's Just The Way It Is' and 'Another Day In Paradise', the lead single released in October 1989.

'Another Day In Paradise' had its origins on 25 May 1987 when Genesis flew from Pittsburg to Washington D.C. during the *Invisible Touch* tour. 'We land from Pittsburgh in snow,' Collins wrote later, 'and as we're coming in from the airport, I ask our driver about the cardboard boxes lined along the pavements in the shadow of the Capitol Building. 'Homeless,' he replies. I'm gobsmacked. Homeless, so many of them, so close to all this wealth and power? An image is planted and fixed in my mind.'

Collins later told *The New York Times* how the song came together: 'It was begun at the piano. I started playing and put it down on a tape so I wouldn't forget it. Then I decided to see what would happen when I started singing. When I began, the words just came out, 'She calls out to the man on the street.' I didn't set out to write a song about the homeless.

Those were just the words I happened to sing. It was only then that I decided that was what the song would be about.'

> I just thought, 'This is one of the wealthiest countries in the world. How can this happen?' It put a bee in my bonnet.'
> Phil Collins, *Rolling Stone*, February 2016

The song was criticised for being heavy-handed and moralistic. 'I know what I meant with 'Another Day In Paradise'', Collins told *Classic Rock* in 2017. 'But people took offence to it because I was rich. What I was saying is that we should all be very appreciative of whatever we've got, as we're all doing better than that. But they all took offence at it.'

The buying public disagreed. 'Another Day In Paradise' gave Phil Collins yet another US number one single. In the UK 'Another Day In Paradise' stalled at number two behind 'All Around The World' by Lisa Stansfield. Collins' song would, however, win a Grammy Award for Record of the Year and the 1990 Brit Award for Best Single.

The album's second single, 'I Wish It Would Rain Down' released in January 1990, would again give Phil Collins a top three in the US and a credible number seven in the UK. The song topped the charts for six weeks in Canada. It was recorded in the same time period (possibly during the same sessions) as Eric Clapton's 'Bad Love' and has a massive production – booming drums, Pino Palladino's fluid bass playing, Clapton's loud guitar and backing from a gospel choir. The nine-minute video is bloody terrible, though.

In the UK, the demo of 'Another Day In Paradise' would be placed as the b-side of 'I Wish It Would Rain Down'. The CD single includes 'You've Been In Love (That Little Bit Too Long)' which pays homage to Phil's beloved Motown.

A demo of 'I Wish It Would Rain Down' – sounding very empty without Clapton – would be released as the b-side of the third single with different songs selected for different markets: 'Something Happened On The Way To Heaven' (UK) and 'Do You Remember?' (US).

'Something Happened On The Way To Heaven' is an up-tempo slice of R&B.

> That was the last song I wrote before I came into the studio and originally, I wrote it for the Four Tops. Since *Buster* we'd done a couple of things together. They said, 'Listen have you got any songs' I said 'I'll try and write

something', so I wrote this song and liked it enough to record the backing track. Danny DeVito called and asked me to write a song for his new film *War Of The Roses* which is a very funny film; very black comedy. He sent me a synopsis of the thing and basically, it's about two people that fall in love with each other but are very, very occupied by what they are doing and they become more and more preoccupied with what they do. That's what the songs about; it's about a relationship falling apart and how at the very last minute, in this particular instance, when they are lying on the floor having almost killed each other, they realise, well he realises that he really loves her and that he made a mistake. But anyway Danny didn't use the song in the film so when the film comes out go see it, it's a great film.
Phil Collins, WEA promo interview, 1989

In the US, 'Something Happened On The Way To Heaven' was the fourth single from the album. It was Collins' last top twenty solo hit – he achieved sixteen top twenty entries in the US between 1981 and 1990 and none thereafter.

'Do You Remember?' started with the working title 'Lionel' – perhaps hinting at the influence of the former Commodores singer Lionel Richie. Collins recalled to *The Mail on Sunday* in March 2010:

It's about how you might meet an old flame in the street and start to reminisce, realising that the reasons for breaking up were maybe not what you remembered. We paint ourselves into corners, and pride doesn't allow us to see things any other way. When I wrote ['Do You Remember?'], people were starting to tire of drum machines, but sometimes they create a hypnotic effect. Real drummers get bored and start getting fancy… and I should know!

The song features backing vocals from Stephen Bishop.

The fourth single in the U.K was 'That's Just The Way It Is', backed by 'Broadway Chorus', a demo of 'Something Happened On The Way To Heaven'. The song, according to Collins, is an anti-war ballad that deals with 'The Troubles' in Northern Ireland, which were not yet resolved in 1989-1990.

Phil Collins in a WEA promo interview in 1989:

It's about Northern Ireland as far as I am concerned. In England, we are used to it all the time … but everywhere else in the world, it's just

> another news report. But if you are living in England and you just sort of constantly see people getting blown to smithereens ... You see newsreels of kids throwing petrol bombs because their brothers throw them and then their Dads throw them and their Dads' Dads and it's just bred, in bred now this violence. And I just thought someone somewhere – and it's got to be from both sides – has got to say, 'Hang on, life means more than this. This has got to stop.

David Crosby again provides harmony vocals. Collins said:

> I'd been a fan of his since the Byrds and I really wanted him because his approach to harmony is unique. He will pick out notes from the air that nobody else would sing. So I had never met him until the Atlantic records 40th-anniversary party. We were backstage and they were rehearsing and I knew Graham Nash and I'd met Stills a couple of times. And I said I've got to meet David he's a big hero of mine. So they introduced me to him and I went backstage and said 'can you sing on my next album' he said 'sure'. He's such a sweet bloke. Because by this time, he got himself sorted out and I just stayed in touch and I sent him a tape when I was in Los Angeles just recently for the album and we had already set it up previously so he knew I was coming in. I sent him a tape of the two songs and he loved them, came in and he was wonderful. We sat down at the piano Because I'd given him a tape he showed me his ideas and he did exactly what I thought he'd do. He came up with these ideas that nobody else would think of.

The final single from *...But Seriously* was the thumping, horn-laden 'Hang In Long Enough'. When asked about the meaning of the song, Collins replied: 'Ambition and greed really. There's two sides of it. One is if you do hang in long enough, you do probably get what you want, but there's an awful lot of carrots being held in front of people to get them to do things. Ambition's a strange thing; it gets people to do very strange things. It makes people do things they wouldn't otherwise do.'

In the UK, the intriguing instrumental 'Around The World In 80 Presets' was the b-side, with another unused song, 'That's How I Feel' on the CD single. A live version of 'Separate Lives' later released on *Serious Hits... Live!* was used in the US. 'Hang In Long Enough' was a minor hit in both territories: not so much of a surprise as it had been first released ten months earlier as the opening track on a multi-selling album.

Of the other songs, 'Find A Way To My Heart' sounds like a cross between 'Take Me Home' and a track from a Disney film – Collins would be hired by the entertainment giant to provide songs for *Tarzan* (1999) and *Brother Bear* (2003). 'All Of My Life' opens with some fat saxophone and features a sincere vocal: evidently, Collins is singing about a life filled with regrets, specifically his relationship with his late father. In the same vein, 'Father To Son' is his own message to his son Simon, then in his late teens. 'Remember what I said. I'll always be with you / Don't forget, just look over your shoulder / I'll be there.' Finally, 'Colours' is an epic mix of Disney and prog rock – late period Genesis with horns.

Collins in the WEA promo interview again, in 1989:

> 'Colours' was always the second half of the song. [It was called] 'Hymn'... for a while. Well, actually, I didn't want to make 'Hymn' a love song; it was just a piano piece and I didn't want to write a love song but I thought it could be used for something more important than that. The idea was like a news documentary-type piece on South Africa, you know, the Ethiopian thing. I wrote it a bit like a Michael Buerk [news report] that started the Band Aid and Live Aid thing off really. And then the second half. I had certain lyrics already and I just thought, as they're both about South Africa, they could work together, so ... under one umbrella, called them 'Colours'.

More than thirty years after its release *...But Seriously* remains one of the fifty all-time best-selling albums, with sales topping 25 million worldwide. It was number one in Australia, Austria, Canada, Denmark, Finland, France, Germany, the Netherlands, New Zealand, Norway, Portugal, Spain, Sweden, Switzerland, the UK and the US. The 2017 re-release adds some demos from pre-production and a handful of b-sides.

Tommy On Stage and the End of the 1980s

If the story is to be believed, Phil Collins would have left Genesis in 1978 to join The Who – had he been asked. Eleven years later, Collins made some amends, appearing twice with The Who at guest-laden performances of their landmark concept album *Tommy*.

'I played Uncle Ernie in *Tommy*,' Collins told *Classic Rock* in 2017. 'Which I loved doing, though it was very politically incorrect – playing a paedophile. But it was great because I was with The Who. I was working with Townshend just after [drummer Keith] Moon died [in 1978], and I said to him, 'Have you got anybody to play the drums? Because I'd love to do it. I'll leave Genesis.' And Pete said, 'Fuck, we've just asked Kenney Jones.' I would have done the job. I would have joined them.'

Collins sang the songs 'Fiddle About' and 'Tommy's Holiday Camp' with sinister gusto, horn-ripped specs and an ill-advised jacket at performances in Los Angeles, on 24 August 1989, and London, on 31 October 1989. Other guests included Billy Idol ('Cousin Kevin'), Elton John ('Pinball Wizard'), Patti Labelle ('Acid Queen') and Steve Winwood ('Eyesight To The Blind'). A TV special and DVD followed.

Phil Collins closed out the 1980s with his only solo live performance of the year on the Arsenio Hall Show, recorded in Los Angeles on 5 December 1989. Joined by Lee Sklar on bass, and a beatific David Crosby on harmony vocals, Collins sang 'That's Just The Way It Is' and 'Another Day In Paradise'. The latter song would hit the top of the charts just before Christmas: the last number one of the eighties on the *Billboard* Hot 100. It would be Collins' eighth top-selling single in the US, all achieved in the previous remarkable six years.

But, to date, it was his last.

Since 1989

> *…But Seriously* is *Billboard*'s first number one album of the nineties. It's the second bestselling album in America in 1990, beaten only by Janet Jackson's *Rhythm Nation 1814*. In the UK, it's number 1 for fifteen weeks in total, winding up [as] the bestselling album of 1990. As the new decade begins I hit the ground running.
> Phil Collins, writing in 2016

Collins would spend most of 1990 touring to promote *…But Seriously*. Genesis' fourteenth studio album, *We Can't Dance*, was recorded between March and September 1991. Released that October, it spawned the big hits 'No Son Of Mine' and 'I Can't Dance', as well as two long tracks harking back to the band's progressive roots: 'Driving The Last Spike' and the magnificent 'Fading Lights'.

The obligatory tour included large outdoor stadia across North America and Europe between May and July 1992, culminating at an immense gig in front of 90,000 lively fans at Knebworth Park. A smaller-scale sixteen date UK tour in October and November ended in Wolverhampton.

Three years after his 1993 album *Both Sides* (another UK number one) and a charity gig with Genesis on 18 September that year, Collins left Genesis to focus on solo work, saying

> I love Genesis, but life was getting very complicated. The more success I had, the more success Genesis had, the more pressures and the more demands there were on my time, and I just had no time for anything else, no personal life. Eventually, Mike and Tony and I got together in my manager's house for lunch to discuss it, and the guys were fine; they realized that it was over for good.

Mike Rutherford wrote in his memoirs:

> Looking back now, I see how strange it was for [Phil] to have gone from being the drummer to the singer. He did it so effortlessly that I don't think Tony or I ever thought much about it at the time, but it had never been part of his plan. All of this meant that when we went for a meeting at Tony Smith's house in Chiddingfold one day in 1996 and Phil said, 'I think I'm going to call it a day,' it wasn't really a surprise. The surprise was that he'd stayed with Genesis as long as he had, after all, that had

happened with his solo career. I still think of him as the drummer who moved to the front rather reluctantly because no one else was going to.

Collins subsequently released *Dance Into The Light* (1996) and *Testify* (2002), as well as writing songs for Disney's *Tarzan* (1999) – for which he received an Oscar for Best Original Song for 'You'll Be In My Heart', his last top ten hit to date in the UK – and *Brother Bear* (2003). Genesis continued with new singer Ray Wilson, releasing the opaque, staid *Calling All Stations* in September 1997. Phil Collins became known as the Tory tax exile who divorced his second wife by fax. He rejoined Genesis in 2000 for an acoustic set at an awards ceremony for their manager Tony Smith – Collins is relaxed, happy and in great voice. The frustratingly short official documentary *Genesis Songbook* provides a few more acoustic performances as bonus features on the DVD, including a spine-chillingly beautiful new version of 'Afterglow'. More substantially, the *Turn It On Again* tour in 2007 returned Genesis to full power with older songs such as 'Follow You Follow Me', 'Ripples', 'I Know What I Like (In My Wardrobe)' and 'The Carpet Crawlers' returning to the set, which focussed principally on songs from 1980 to 1992. An estimated half a million fans saw their concert at the Circus Maximus in Rome on 14 July 2007. Their final date was at the Hollywood Bowl on 13 October 2007. That, seemingly, was all.

Phil Collins' most recent solo album, 2010's *Going Back*, features covers of 1960s Motown and soul standards. He retired in 2011.

I just wanted to get off the roundabout. I had had enough, frankly. I wanted to be written out of my own script. There were too many things stuck to me that I couldn't get rid of. It seemed that the only way I could stop this was to stop and start again. I stopped. I'm yet to start again.
Phil Collins, *The Guardian*, 2016

I retired so I could be at home with the kids. Then my wife left me and took the kids – they moved to Miami – so I found myself in a void with no work. But I didn't really want to work, and the kids weren't there. I had a big hole in my life and I started drinking. And I wanted to stop, so I could be with my kids. I also wanted to stop so that I could maybe do something else – I didn't know what – though I felt I deserved the right to do nothing. All this stuff happened. The ear thing was in 2000 – I lost my hearing in my left ear – and then [waves arm painfully] the arm [a

spinal injury affected his nerves in 2009, making it impossible for him to play the drums]. I had various operations. I still can't play, but it's better than it was. I'm a man of my word, but, at the same time, there's a hole where that used to be and I might as well do something.
Phil Collins, *Classic Rock*, 2017.

He published his extremely frank memoirs in 2016. Tentatively returning to live performances, 'Against All Odds (Take A Look At Me Now)' on *The Jonathon Ross Show* that October introduced a visibly aged, physically frail and vocally weakened performer. Fifty years of drumming, back operations, perpetual overwork and ill-health exacerbated by a fall necessitated Collins needing to walk with a stick.

Undeterred, the *Not Dead Yet* tour ran intermittently between June 2017 and October 2019. Over the course of ninety-seven shows, Collins' voice and health improved, though still much diminished. He was confident enough to include two Genesis songs in his set, including a crowd-pleasing 'Throwing It All Away' and an emotional reading of 'Follow You Follow Me'. Collins' son Nic, sitting behind the drums, made the old man proud. Collins was supported on several dates by his pal Mike Rutherford's band Mike + The Mechanics and, thrillingly, the old friends would sometimes share the stage.

Collins and his Genesis bandmates had met in London in June 2017, and once again, the idea to tour as a band was mooted. Finally, in January 2020, Collins, Rutherford and Banks regrouped for two weeks rehearsal in New York.

'I think it's a natural moment,' Mike Rutherford told BBC Radio 2. 'It's happened very naturally. Phil's been out on tour doing his stuff and it sort of seemed ... the natural moment to have a conversation about it. We're all good friends, we're all above grass and here we are.'

'New York was a good experience,' noted manager Tony Smith. 'Everyone thought that we could do it, that it would work. So at that point, we said OK, let's start planning'.

The tour was announced on 4 March 2020 and full production rehearsals commenced in October and November. Initially, ten dates were planned in Ireland and the UK between 16 November and 11 December 2020, but the tour was postponed to September-October 2021 in response to the COVID-19 pandemic. Long-time lieutenant Daryl Stuermer provided bass and guitar – forty-three years after his first dates with Genesis – and Collins' precociously talented son Nic skilfully subbed for his ailing father behind the drums. Backing vocalists Daniel Pearce and Patrick Smyth beefed up Collins' reduced vocal capacity. 'When you're struggling with the voice, it's very difficult. [The backing vocalists] take a weight off my shoulders,' Collins stated in an hour-long PBS documentary filmed in late 2020 and broadcast in September 2021. Interviews with the band – Collins is obviously physically fragile but has a sparkle in his eyes – joined snippets of the band rehearsing 'That's All', 'Carpet Crawlers', 'Mama', '...In That Quiet Earth', 'Land Of Confusion', 'Domino' and 'Throwing It All Away'. Nic Collins barely draws breath.

'I'm physically challenged a bit, which is frustrating,' Phil told *BBC Breakfast* on 9 September, two weeks before the tour commenced. 'I'd love to be playing up there with my son. I can barely hold a stick. We're all men of our age. I think this probably is putting Genesis to bed. I don't know if I want to go out on the road anymore.' A weary Collins looked and sounded ten years older than his 70 years.

A new double CD, 4 LP 'best-of' album named after the tour was released a few days ahead of the opening date at the Utilita Arena in Birmingham. This generated considerable online debate: would these songs comprise the band's setlist for the tour?

The answer was 'yes it would', as the newly-rejuvenated band performed a resolute set, with a few surprises, replicating the CD almost track-for-track: 'Duke's Intro', 'Turn It On Again', 'Mama', 'Land Of Confusion', 'Home By The Sea / Second Home By The Sea' then 'Fading Lights' with instrumental portions of 'The Cinema Show' and '…In That Quiet Earth', and the always magnificent 'Afterglow'. A short 'unplugged' set gave us 'That's All', a new arrangement of 'The Lamb Lies Down On Broadway', then 'Follow You Follow Me'. The very welcome return of 'Duchess', performed for the first time since 1981, opened a flawless section comprising 'No Son Of Mine', an instrumental section of 'Fifth of Fifth', 'I Know What I Like (In Your Wardrobe)', a snippet of 'Stagnation', 'Domino' and 'Throwing It All Away'. The show concluded with 'Tonight, Tonight, Tonight' and, inevitably, 'Invisible Touch'. Encores comprised 'I Can't Dance', the first verse of 'Dancing With The Moonlit Knight' and an emotional 'Carpet Crawlers'.

Collins, despite his fading voice and diminished physicality, commanded attention, air drumming and conducting, charisma fully intact.

Your author saw the tour at the Liverpool Arena on 4 October 2021. Much of the show was magnificent, even if many people chose to head to the bar during 'Fading Lights' and had obviously never previously heard the glorious 'Duchess'.

Epilogue

Perpetually disliked by critics and often hounded by the British popular press, Phil Collins has enjoyed incredible success, especially in the 1980s. Notably, he is one of only three recording artists who have sold over one hundred million records worldwide, both as a solo artist and as a principal member of a band. Here he joins an elite group with Paul McCartney and Michael Jackson. Collins has won eight Grammy Awards, six Brit Awards (winning Best British Male Artist three times), two Golden Globe Awards, one Academy Award and six Ivor Novellos.

In a way, Phil Collins has enjoyed two, three, or four parallel careers: as a drummer, songwriter, band member, session musician, producer, and occasional actor. You cannot deny that he was everywhere in the 1980s, and his commercial success in that decade was astonishing. But the payoff is that his health and three marriages have been damaged or destroyed: a high price for anyone. The shocked response to Collins' aged appearance in 2021 perhaps confirms how firmly the image of him in the 1980s is fixed in the public consciousness.

> Like the story that we wish was never ending
> We know some time we must reach that final page
> And still we carry on just pretending
> That there'll always be just one more day to go
>
> So far away, away, fading distant lights
> Leaving us all behind, lost in a changing world
> And you know that these are the days of our lives
> So remember...

Although it's unlikely that the best is to come – and a positive reassessment of his remarkable 50-year career is long overdue – we should remain grateful, in his own words, that he's not dead yet.

> Phil Collins requires you to hold many seemingly opposing thoughts in your head at all times. He's historically underrated as a musician and singer, though lately, he might also be a little overrated, too. *No Jacket Required* and *Invisible Touch* sound dated, and but they're also two of the best and most lasting pop albums of the '80s. I suspect he's both a nice guy and a bit of a bastard—insecure and humble as well as conceited

and megalomaniacal. He's the Cartesian pop star, eternally resisting absolutism. Take a look at Phil Collins now. There's just an empty space, waiting to be filled.
Steven Hyden, *The Ringer*, 2018

Hello, I must be going
I cannot stay
I came to say
I must be going
I'm glad I came
But just the same
I must be going, la-la!
Bert Kalmar and Harry Ruby, 1930

Phil Collins On Tour and On Record 1980-1989

1980

March-May 1980 – Duke tour (UK)
May-June 1980 – Duke tour (US)

Genesis – *Duke*
Peter Gabriel – *Peter Gabriel*
Mike Oldfield – *QE2*
John Martyn – *Grace and Danger*

1981

11-12 September 1981 – The Secret Policeman's Other Ball
September-November 1981 – Abacab Tour (Europe)
November-December 1981 – Abacab Tour (North America)
December 1981 – Abacab Tour (UK)

Jack Lancaster – *Skinningrove Bay*
Brian Chatton – *Playing For Time*
Rupert Hine – *Immunity*
Phil Collins – *Face Value*
John Martyn – *Glorious Fool*
Genesis – *Abacab*
Genesis – *3 x 3* EP

1982

7 July 1982 – Prince's Trust Rock Gala
November 1982 – Hello, I Must Be Going! Tour (Europe and UK)
December 1982 – Hello, I Must Be Going! Tour (US)

Robert Plant – *Pictures At Eleven*
Frida – *Frida*
Gary Brooker – *Lead Me To The Water*
Rupert Hine – *Waving Not Drowning*
Ralph McTell – *Water Of Dreams*
Marti Webb – *I'm Not That Kind Of Girl*
Genesis – *Three Sides Live*
Phil Collins – *Hello, I Must Be Going!*

1983

January-February 1983 – Hello, I Must Be Going! Tour (US)
August-October 1982 – with Robert Plant (US)
November-December 1983 – Mama tour (US)

Robert Plant – *The Principle of Moments*
Al Di Meola – *Scenario*
Adam Ant – *Strip*
Genesis – *Genesis*

1984

January-February 1984 – Mama tour (US)
February 1984 – Mama tour (UK)

Phil Collins – 'Against All Odds (Take A Look At Me Now)'
Eric Clapton – *Behind The Sun*
Philip Bailey – *Chinese Wall*
Phil Collins – *No Jacket Required*
Band Aid – 'Do They Know It's Christmas?'

1985

February-March 1985 – No Jacket Required tour (Europe)
March-April 1985 – No Jacket Required tour (Oceania and Japan)
May-July 1985 – No Jacket Required tour (North America)
13 July 1985 – Live Aid, London and Philadelphia

Phil Collins and Marilyn Martin – 'Separate Lives'

1986

20 June 1986 – Prince's Trust Rock Gala
July 1986 – with Eric Clapton (Europe and UK)
September-December 1986 – Invisible Touch tour (North America, Oceania)

Howard Jones – 'No One Is To Blame'
Genesis – *Invisible Touch*
Eric Clapton – *August*
Paul McCartney – *Press To Play*
Tina Turner – *Break Every Rule*

Phil Bailey – *Inside Out*
Chaka Khan – *Destiny*

1987

January-March 1987 – Invisible Touch tour (US, Japan)
April 1987 – with Eric Clapton (US)
May-July 1987 – Invisible Touch tour (US, Europe, UK)
5 June 1987 – Princes Trust Rock Gala

Phil Collins – *12"ers*

1988

14 May 1988 – Atlantic Records' 40th Anniversary Concert

Phil Collins – 'A Groovy Kind Of Love', 'Two Hearts'
Boys Don't Cry – *Boys Don't Cry*
The Four Tops – 'Loco In Acapulco'
Mike + The Mechanics – *The Living Years*

1989

24 August 1989 – with The Who
31 October 1989 – with The Who

Stephen Bishop – *Bowling In Paris*
Tears For Fears – *Seeds Of Love*
Eric Clapton – *Journeyman*
Phil Collins – *...But Seriously*

Bibliography

Aldous, S., *The Songs of Genesis: A Complete Guide to the Studio Recordings* (McFarland, Jefferson, 2020)
Banks, Collins et al. *Genesis: Chapter and Verse* (Weidenfeld & Nicolson, London, 2007)
Barnes, M., *A New Day Yesterday* (Omnibus Press, London, 2020)
Bowler. D., and Dray, B., *Genesis A Biography* (Sidgwick and Jackson, London, 1992)
Burns, R., *Experiencing Progressive Rock: A Listener's Companion* (Rowman & Littlefield, Lanham, 2018)
Chatton, B., *Rolling With Rock Royalty* (self-published, 2020)
Clapton, E., *Eric Clapton: The Autobiography* (Cornerstone, London, 2010)
Coleman, R., *Phil Collins The Definitive Biography* (Simon & Schuster, London, 1997)
Collins, P., *Not Dead Yet: The Autobiography* (Cornerstone, London, 2016)
Hann, M., *Phil Collins – Plays Well With Others* sleeve notes (Rhino, 2018)
Hegerty, P. and Halliwell, H., *Beyond and Before: Progressive Rock Since The 1960s* (Contunuum, London, 2011)
Hyden, S., *Twilight of the Gods: A Journey to the End of Classic Rock* (Dey Street Books, New York, 2018)
Kamin, P. and Goddard, P., *Genesis: Peter Gabriel, Phil Collins & Beyond* (Stoddard, London, 1984)
Macfarlane, S., *On Track… Genesis – Every Album, Every Song* (Sonicbond, Tewksbury, 2019)
Madinger, C. and Easter, M., *Eight Arms To Hold You: The Solo Beatles Compendium* (44 1 Productions Inc, 2001)
Marks, C. and Tannenbaum, R., *I Want My MTV* (Penguin, London, 2011)
Massey, H., *Behind The Glass, Volume 1* (Hal Leonard, San Francisco, 2000)
- *Behind The Glass, Volume 2* (Hal Leonard, San Francisco, 2009)
- *The Great British Recording Studios* (Hal Leonard, Milwaukee, 2015)
Oldfield, M., *Changeling* (Virgin Books, London, 2007)
Palm, C., *The Real Story of Abba: Bright Lights, Dark Shadows* (Omnibus Press, London, 2014)
Platts, R., *Genesis: Behind The Lines: 1967–2007* (Collector's Guide Publishing, Burlington, Ontario, 2007)

Rees, P., *Robert Plant: A Life* (HarperCollins, London, 2013)
Romano, W., *Prog Rock FAQ* (Backbeat, London, 2014)
Rutherford. M., *The Living Years* (Constable, London, 2014)
Thompson, G., *Small Hours: The Long Night of John Martyn* (Omnibus Press, London, 2020)
Weigel, D., *The Show That Never Ends: The Rise And Fall Of Prog Rock* (W.W. Norton, New York, 2017)
Welch, C., *Genesis: The Complete Guide To Their Music* (Omnibus Press, London, 2005)
Yard, R., *Mike Oldfield: Every Album Every Song* (Sonicbond, Tewksbury, 2020)

On Track series

Alan Parsons Project – Steve Swift 978-1-78952-154-2
Tori Amos – Lisa Torem 978-1-78952-142-9
Asia – Peter Braidis 978-1-78952-099-6
Badfinger – Robert Day-Webb 978-1-878952-176-4
Barclay James Harvest – Keith and Monica Domone 978-1-78952-067-5
The Beatles – Andrew Wild 978-1-78952-009-5
The Beatles Solo 1969-1980 – Andrew Wild 978-1-78952-030-9
Blue Oyster Cult – Jacob Holm-Lupo 978-1-78952-007-1
Blur – Matt Bishop 978-178952-164-1
Marc Bolan and T.Rex – Peter Gallagher 978-1-78952-124-5
Kate Bush – Bill Thomas 978-1-78952-097-2
Camel – Hamish Kuzminski 978-1-78952-040-8
Caravan – Andy Boot 978-1-78952-127-6
Cardiacs – Eric Benac 978-1-78952-131-3
Eric Clapton Solo – Andrew Wild 978-1-78952-141-2
The Clash – Nick Assirati 978-1-78952-077-4
Crosby, Stills and Nash – Andrew Wild 978-1-78952-039-2
The Damned – Morgan Brown 978-1-78952-136-8
Deep Purple and Rainbow 1968-79 – Steve Pilkington 978-1-78952-002-6
Dire Straits – Andrew Wild 978-1-78952-044-6
The Doors – Tony Thompson 978-1-78952-137-5
Dream Theater – Jordan Blum 978-1-78952-050-7
Electric Light Orchestra – Barry Delve 978-1-78952-152-8
Elvis Costello and The Attractions – Georg Purvis 978-1-78952-129-0
Emerson Lake and Palmer – Mike Goode 978-1-78952-000-2
Fairport Convention – Kevan Furbank 978-1-78952-051-4
Peter Gabriel – Graeme Scarfe 978-1-78952-138-2
Genesis – Stuart MacFarlane 978-1-78952-005-7
Gentle Giant – Gary Steel 978-1-78952-058-3
Gong – Kevan Furbank 978-1-78952-082-8
Hall and Oates – Ian Abrahams 978-1-78952-167-2
Hawkwind – Duncan Harris 978-1-78952-052-1
Peter Hammill – Richard Rees Jones 978-1-78952-163-4
Roy Harper – Opher Goodwin 978-1-78952-130-6
Jimi Hendrix – Emma Stott 978-1-78952-175-7
The Hollies – Andrew Darlington 978-1-78952-159-7
Iron Maiden – Steve Pilkington 978-1-78952-061-3
Jefferson Airplane – Richard Butterworth 978-1-78952-143-6
Jethro Tull – Jordan Blum 978-1-78952-016-3
Elton John in the 1970s – Peter Kearns 978-1-78952-034-7
The Incredible String Band – Tim Moon 978-1-78952-107-8
Iron Maiden – Steve Pilkington 978-1-78952-061-3
Judas Priest – John Tucker 978-1-78952-018-7
Kansas – Kevin Cummings 978-1-78952-057-6
The Kinks – Martin Hutchinson 978-1-78952-172-6
Korn – Matt Karpe 978-1-78952-153-5
Led Zeppelin – Steve Pilkington 978-1-78952-151-1
Level 42 – Matt Philips 978-1-78952-102-3
Little Feat – 978-1-78952-168-9
Aimee Mann – Jez Rowden 978-1-78952-036-1
Joni Mitchell – Peter Kearns 978-1-78952-081-1
The Moody Blues – Geoffrey Feakes 978-1-78952-042-2
Motorhead – Duncan Harris 978-1-78952-173-3
Mike Oldfield – Ryan Yard 978-1-78952-060-6
Opeth – Jordan Blum 978-1-78-952-166-5
Tom Petty – Richard James 978-1-78952-128-3
Porcupine Tree – Nick Holmes 978-1-78952-144-3
Queen – Andrew Wild 978-1-78952-003-3
Radiohead – William Allen 978-1-78952-149-8
Renaissance – David Detmer 978-1-78952-062-0
The Rolling Stones 1963-80 – Steve Pilkington 978-1-78952-017-0
The Smiths and Morrissey – Tommy Gunnarsson 978-1-78952-140-5
Status Quo the Frantic Four Years – Richard James 978-1-78952-160-3
Steely Dan – Jez Rowden 978-1-78952-043-9
Steve Hackett – Geoffrey Feakes 978-1-78952-098-9
Thin Lizzy – Graeme Stroud 978-1-78952-064-4
Toto – Jacob Holm-Lupo 978-1-78952-019-4

U2 – Eoghan Lyng 978-1-78952-078-1
UFO – Richard James 978-1-78952-073-6
The Who – Geoffrey Feakes
978-1-78952-076-7
Roy Wood and the Move – James R Turner
978-1-78952-008-8
Van Der Graaf Generator – Dan Coffey
978-1-78952-031-6
Yes – Stephen Lambe 978-1-78952-001-9
Frank Zappa 1966 to 1979 – Eric Benac
978-1-78952-033-0
Warren Zevon – Peter Gallagher
978-1-78952-170-2
10CC – Peter Kearns 978-1-78952-054-5

Decades Series
The Bee Gees in the 1960s –
Andrew Mon Hughes et al 978-1-78952-148-1
The Bee Gees in the 1970s –
Andrew Mon Hughes et al 978-1-78952-179-5
Black Sabbath in the 1970s – Chris Sutton
978-1-78952-171-9
Britpop – Peter Richard Adams and Matt Pooler
978-1-78952-169-6
Alice Cooper in the 1970s – Chris Sutton
978-1-78952-104-7
Curved Air in the 1970s – Laura Shenton
978-1-78952-069-9
Bob Dylan in the 1980s – Don Klees
978-1-78952-157-3
Fleetwood Mac in the 1970s – Andrew Wild
978-1-78952-105-4
Focus in the 1970s – Stephen Lambe
978-1-78952-079-8
Free and Bad Company in the 1970s –
John Van der Kiste 978-1-78952-178-8
Genesis in the 1970s – Bill Thomas
978178952-146-7
George Harrison in the 1970s – Eoghan Lyng
978-1-78952-174-0
Marillion in the 1980s – Nathaniel Webb
978-1-78952-065-1
Mott the Hoople and Ian Hunter in the 1970s –
John Van der Kiste 978-1-78-952-162-7
Pink Floyd In The 1970s – Georg Purvis
978-1-78952-072-9
Tangerine Dream in the 1970s –
Stephen Palmer 978-1-78952-161-0
The Sweet in the 1970s – Darren Johnson
978-1-78952-139-9
Uriah Heep in the 1970s – Steve Pilkington
978-1-78952-103-0
Yes in the 1980s – Stephen Lambe with David
Watkinson 978-1-78952-125-2

On Screen series
Carry On… – Stephen Lambe 978-1-78952-004-0
David Cronenberg – Patrick Chapman
978-1-78952-071-2
Doctor Who: The David Tennant Years –
Jamie Hailstone 978-1-78952-066-8
James Bond – Andrew Wild –
978-1-78952-010-1
Monty Python – Steve Pilkington
978-1-78952-047-7
Seinfeld Seasons 1 to 5 – Stephen Lambe
978-1-78952-012-5

Other Books
1967: A Year In Psychedelic Rock – Kevan
Furbank
978-1-78952-155-9
1970: A Year In Rock – John Van der Kiste
978-1-78952-147-4
1973: The Golden Year of Progressive Rock
978-1-78952-165-8
Babysitting A Band On The Rocks –
G.D. Praetorius 978-1-78952-106-1
Eric Clapton Sessions – Andrew Wild
978-1-78952-177-1
Derek Taylor: For Your Radioactive Children –
Andrew Darlington 978-1-78952-038-5
The Golden Road: The Recording History of The
Grateful Dead –
John Kilbride 978-1-78952-156-6
Iggy and The Stooges On Stage 1967-1974 –
Per Nilsen 978-1-78952-101-6
Jon Anderson and the Warriors – the road to Yes
– David Watkinson 978-1-78952-059-0
Nu Metal: A Definitive Guide – Matt Karpe
978-1-78952-063-7
Tommy Bolin: In and Out of Deep Purple –
Laura Shenton 978-1-78952-070-5
Maximum Darkness – Deke Leonard
978-1-78952-048-4
Maybe I Should've Stayed In Bed –
Deke Leonard 978-1-78952-053-8
The Twang Dynasty – Deke Leonard
978-1-78952-049-1

and many more to come!